REAL WOMEN WRITE:

Growing / Older

FOREWORD BY
Susan Wittig Albert

EDITED BY
Susan F. Schoch

**SHARING STORIES, SHARING LIVES
IN PROSE AND POETRY FROM
STORY CIRCLE NETWORK**

A Publication of Story Circle Network

Real Women Write: Growing / Older
Sharing Stories, Sharing Lives
in Prose and Poetry from Story Circle Network
Volume 18, 2019

ISBN: 978-0-9795329-5-5

Story Circle Network
723 W University Ave #300-234
Georgetown, TX 78626

www.storycircle.org

Real Women Write is an annual anthology of writing by Story Circle Network members, including nonfiction, fiction, and poetry. It appears in December in both print and digital forms, showcasing the talent and creativity of our own writing women.

Story Circle Network values every woman's story, and in *Real Women Write* we publish writing about both the individual life in all its uniqueness, and a woman's life as it's understood by all women.

Foreword by Susan Wittig Albert

Edited by Susan F. Schoch

Cover image, interior design, and technical support by Sherry Wachter

"We have to make myths of our lives…

if we do, then every grief or inexplicable seizure by weather,

woe, or work can—if we discipline ourselves and think hard

enough—be turned to account, be made to yield further insight

into what it is to be alive, to be a human being."

— May Sarton

CONTENTS

vii FOREWORD   Susan Wittig Albert

xi FROM THE EDITOR   Susan F. Schoch

F = Fiction   NF = Nonfiction   P = Poetry

1 She Can Be Taught: My New Five-Second Rule   NF   Jeanne Baker Guy

3 Loose Leaf Pages   P   Bonnie Watkins

4 Vernie   NF   Shawn M. LaTorre

6 Shooting Stars   P   Margaret Dubay Mikus

7 What Went Unsaid   P   Pat Anthony

8 Anticipating a Zadie   NF   Marlene B. Samuels

11 Camp Tee Ata   NF   Lois Ann Bull

14 The Swooper   NF   Rollyn Carlson

17 B+   NF   Jane Gragg Lewis

18 Ventriloquist for Jesus   NF   Claire Butler

21 Memorializing Aunt Maggie   NF   Debra Dolan

23 Lost Childhood   NF   Lois Ann Bull

25 Why I Didn't Become a Young Writer   NF   Deborah L. Bean

WRITERS IN THE SPOTLIGHT

28 Spotlight on Pat Bean   Susan F. Schoch

31 The Little Girl in the Photograph   NF   Pat Bean

33 Angel's Landing   NF   Pat Bean

35 Two Mistakes and a Surprise   NF   Pat Bean

37 I am 80   NF   Pat Bean

40 Must Have Been the Stars   NF   Ariela Zucker

42 Spring Again   P   Shelley Johnson Carey

43 Pangs   NF   Marilea C. Rabasa

47 The Casting   P   Katelynn Butler

49 Westerns   P   Claire McCabe

50 Make It Happen   F   Marilyn H. Collins

53 Starting Over   NF   Charlotte Wlodkowski

54 Finding Buster   NF   Jude Walsh

56 One Woman's Life   NF   Marilyn H. Collins

59 Amelia, the WASP, and Me   NF   Sarah Byrn Rickman

62 A Tale of Two Committees   NF   Susan D. Corbin

65 A Small Gift Strikes the Right Chord   NF   Lisa Braxton

68 The Lampadedromia   NF   Sara Etgen-Baker

71 Conversation   P   Jane Gragg Lewis

72 Aging – For Bella, For All Of Us P   Jazz Jaeschke Kendrick
73 Let Go, Hold On P   Jazz Jaeschke Kendrick
74 Tuesday at my Local Grocery Store F   Ann Haas
76 Summering After Fifty P   Pat Anthony
77 Advice to My Younger Self NF   Jo Virgil
78 Marking Time P   Nancilynn Saylor
79 Our Chee Experience NF   Betsy Boyd
81 Aging Goddesses P   Madeline Sharples
82 Impermanence of Life P   Mary Jo West
83 Paradise Lost NF   Linda D. Menicucci
85 Act Your Age F   Penelope Starr
87 Role Reversal NF   Betsy Boyd
89 Lavender Dreams NF   Marjorie Witt
92 Dinner with the Butterfly Whisperer NF   Sara Etgen-Baker
95 When I Am Eighty NF   Jeanne Zeeb-Schecter
97 Scallops P   Juliana Lightle
98 Awakened Senses NF   Susan Flemr
100 Give Me a Head with Hair NF   Bonnie Watkins
102 Homage to My Breasts P   Maya Lazarus
103 Things I've Thought About P   Carol J. Wechsler Blatter
103 Finding My Roots: Growing Older NF   Jo Virgil
104 Anti-aging Cream P   Madeline Sharples
105 Aging P   Juliana Lightle
106 Carpe Diem, Old Friend NF   Sarah Fine
107 "Swift as the Wild Goose Flies" NF   Suzanne Adam
110 A Time for Everything P   Ariela Zucker
110 Ruby NF   Janice Airhart
114 From the Stars P   Margaret Dubay Mikus
115 The Best of Times NF   Mary Jo Doig
118 Retrospective P   Linda D. Menicucci
119 Towing a Jeep P   Maya Lazarus
120 Dream Reflections NF   Carol Toole

122 ABOUT THE CONTRIBUTORS
132 ABOUT THE EDITOR
133 ABOUT STORY CIRCLE NETWORK:
    FOR WOMEN WITH STORIES TO TELL
135 BOOKS PUBLISHED BY STORY CIRCLE NETWORK

FOREWORD

WHY WOMEN'S STORIES MATTER
by Susan Wittig Albert

Each of the stories in this anthology is a woman's story about a woman's life, and that's what makes it both special and important. It's not the eloquent prose or poetry (although each pieces has its own eloquence, in its own voice). Nor is it breathtaking action or compelling characterizations or exotic settings or a twisty ending. Each story is important because, quite simply, it is a story about what happened to a woman and what she thought or felt about it, and what happened next, and after that. And what she learned from it, and why, and how that was important to her. Stories matter. Women's stories matter.

Think for a moment about how many women's stories have been lost over the millennia of human history. Oh, we have plenty of men's stories about women, although these are almost exclusively about "important" women: important because they are the wives, daughters, mothers, and mistresses of "important" men. What has been lost are stories about ordinary women leading ordinary lives, doing the things that have kept families together, businesses operating, communities thriving. Until the last hundred years or so and with a few exceptions (Hildegard of Bingen comes to mind), we don't have women's stories about their creative lives, their imaginative lives, their dreams.

We need to tell our stories. We need to tell them so that the women who follow us will know what our lives were really like, and know that their mothers and grandmothers and great-grandmothers were more than just characters in men's tales, that we were dimensional, intentional persons with minds of our own, wills of our own, hopes of our own. But these personal stories are by necessity political stories, as well. That is, they are stories about power: who has it and how it is used and abused, as every woman with a #MeToo story will tell you.

But if we feel an urgent social and political need to tell our true stories, we also feel, often unconsciously, an urgent psychological need. Every day, all around the globe, women sit together in kitchens and classrooms, on park benches and at office desks, around tables in cafes and in chat rooms on the internet, telling their stories, often embodying their truths in fiction. "I have to do this," a woman in one of my writing classes said. "I'm afraid that if I don't tell my story, I won't be real!"

As many of the stories in this anthology demonstrate, this storytelling work is remarkably, rewardingly healthy. As we reveal ourselves in story—whether in memoir, fiction, or poetry—we become aware of the continuing core of our being under the fragmenting surface of our experience. As we become conscious of the multifaceted, multichaptered "I" who is the storyteller, we can discover the paradoxical and even contradictory versions of ourselves that we create for different occasions, different audiences—and the threads that weave all these versions into one whole. We can see how we have grown: grown older, yes, but also grown wiser, more tolerant and flexible, more transparent.

There is a certain circular truth here, don't you think? As we learn to experience ourselves as tellers of our life's story, we realize that what we understand and imagine about ourselves is a story. It is only one way (not the only way) of representing our experience, of composing and recomposing, of inventing and reinventing ourselves. Seeing our stories as stories—and hence open to radical revision and reimagining—can help us heal from the wounds that experience inflicts upon us. Finding ourselves as writers, we can find ourselves to be the authors of our lives.

Once we understand this, we see that the ordinary stories of our daily lives, so rich with trial and error, so deeply rooted in the here-and-now, so embodied and real and various—these ordinary stories are truly extraordinary. When we frame the small moments of life in our stories, we can begin to see and feel their larger significance as part of the work that is given to each of us to do. As you read the pieces collected in this anthology, think of that, for this is where learning and growing happens—whether we are growing abler or more disabled, wiser or more naive, trusting or more questioning.

At Story Circle, because we believe in the importance of women's stories, our publication program is one of the most important programs we offer. Members can publish their work in our quarterly Journal, on our website, through our writing competitions, and in our occasional publications (such as our books: *What Wildness Is This* and *With Courage and Common Sense*). This anthology, the eighteenth in our long series, is part of that enduring commitment, and we are glad to be sharing it, for the first time, in book form. Story Circle also sponsors the annual Sarton Book Awards, and Story Circle Book Reviews, as well as conferences, writing retreats, and online classes that support women's writing. Over and over again, in all the ways we can think of, we say that women's stories must be told.

My story, your story, our stories. You and I are the only ones who can tell them, because we are the ones who have lived them, and because they are true.

SUSAN WITTIG ALBERT
Founder and President Emerita
Story Circle Network

FROM THE EDITOR

December, 2019

Welcome to the eighteenth edition of Story Circle Network's annual anthology, *Real Women Write: Sharing Stories, Sharing Lives.* We're proud to present this extraordinary collection of fiction, nonfiction, and poetry by our members.

Volume 18 is an edition of changes. We are changing our publication methods, moving to a format that will be available on Amazon as an e-book and a print-on-demand paperback. This will give many more readers an opportunity to discover Story Circle and its remarkable women's writing, and will increase exposure for our authors, as well. Sherry Wachter, a longtime SCN member and gifted teacher, author, and artist, has been invaluable in making this transition technically possible. Sherry also created our beautiful cover and designed the interior. This issue will be the foundation for many to come, and we're very grateful for her expert and enthusiastic efforts.

Another change was the suggestion, for the first time, of a topic or theme for this issue: Growing / Older. It's a broad subject, since all our lives we are growing and growing older, and so is all the life around us. In the first years, growing older means enormous leaps forward in abilities, understanding, physical prowess. In later years, it may mean physical failings, losing friends, new careers, greater freedom. We asked our members to explore the topic in terms of the change and growth in every life at any stage.

As always, members were free to write on any topic for *Real Women Write 2019*, but they responded strongly to this theme, giving us a wide range of insightful and vulnerable responses. A woman, a dog, a star—all have their own stages and signs of the growth that comes as time passes. From childhood memories to midlife dreams to the hard-won wisdom of advanced age, these authors have plumbed their lives in stories, essays, and poems. Their work will intrigue and inspire you.

While *RWW* includes a large sampling of entries received, space restricts our selections, and so do other editorial considerations, such as subject, imagery, style, and coherence. We work hard to choose the best writing—fresh, engaging, worth your time—while balancing opportunities for writers of varied experience. With a light hand, we edit selections for spelling, punctuation, grammar, and consistency of style, always maintaining the writer's voice as much as possible. Though we're not able to share all the good work that is submitted, every entry is greatly appreciated, for each one speaks from the heart. And each one may reveal something to you—a deeper meaning, greater understanding, or unexpected confirmation.

Of course, some things don't change. SCN's mission is consistently to help women grow through writing, and to generate greater awareness of the significance of women's lived experience and their creativity. In the diverse and meaningful works you will find here, that mission is again fulfilled, this time through the exploration of a powerful common life event.

Speaking personally, editing this collection is always a tremendous honor, a new experience every time, and one that has growth in it for me. Yet getting it out to the world is a major group effort. Thanks go to all of our contributors for sharing themselves so bravely and well. Also, gratitude to the officers and board of Story Circle, especially our intrepid president, Jeanne Guy, for recognizing the value of publication and supporting numerous avenues for our members. Special thanks to Teresa Lynn and Abby Morris for superb administrative help. And as always, appreciation to Susan Wittig Albert, SCN's founder and president emerita, and expert consultant on every stage of creating this anthology. She continues to be an engine for moving our organization forward and a mentor to many of us word-loving women.

Story Circle Network and *Real Women Write* keep us moving ahead on our authentic paths. That kind of support lifts our voices and turns them into a life-changing chorus. Here, for the eighteenth time, are SCN women singing out!

SUSAN SCHOCH, EDITOR
Real Women Write: Growing / Older

SHE CAN BE TAUGHT:
MY NEW FIVE-SECOND RULE

Jeanne Baker Guy

Older is one thing. Growing is another.

First, an "older" story.

Let's say I'm seventy-two. Okay, I am seventy-two. Normally I'm happy about my age and the fact that I've lived this long. I have one regret: seventy-two equates to that magic word: old. Just like when I met an eye surgeon for the first time a few months back. Having reviewed my chart before entering the room, he paid me an intended compliment when he shook my hand and said, "Have to confess, I thought I was meeting a much older woman." With great wit, tinged with snarkiness, I told him I'd purposely left my walker in the waiting room.

Though the guy made my day, the whole age thing annoys me. I've annoyed myself with my own thinking about "old" people.

Several years ago, I facilitated a retreat on Whidbey Island off the coast of Seattle. I received a registration from an "elderly" woman and my first thought was, "Oh my gosh, how will she manage the travel arrangements, the shuttle, the ferry, etc., to get here? "

She was seventy-two. Now that I'm seventy-two, I have to ask myself, what was I thinking?

Aging can be a struggle.

———

So, what is growing? How am I, at the age of seventy-two, growing?

By being open to change and experiencing new ways of thinking. I've gained in wisdom recently not because I'm old—there, I've said it—but because I've experienced something new: the 5-Second Rule.

The only five-second rule I've ever known about was the one where if you dropped food on the floor, you had five seconds to pick it up and blow the dust or dirt off before dropping it in your mouth.

That's not to say I don't still do that, but, at my age (did I mention I'm seventy-two?), I've learned something new. I watched a "non-motivational" YouTube video on how to stop procrastinating, and voilá! It seems to be working.

Mel Robbins (author of The 5 Second Rule) says I have about a five-second window from a) the moment I know (have knowledge) that I should do something, to b) making the decision to do it—before my brain steps in and talks me out of it.

All day long I have choices. If I don't take action, my brain kicks in and sabotages me.

I've recently lost about fifteen pounds after hooking up with myfitnesspal.com, thanks to my grown son and daughter. I log in daily to the app, track my food, water intake, weight, and exercise, all the while being encouraged and supported by my kids, who are also on the app.

Having been an avid walker for thirty years, I love cardio. The thought of strength training, on the other hand, causes me to do the laundry, or clean the kitty litter—anything but picking up those free weights. I avoid doing that which "at my age" would serve me well.

Why is it that we know what we should do but we procrastinate or totally avoid doing what inevitably would make us stronger and feel better?

It's not motivation I'm missing. It's action. I've always believed that motion is lotion, so this makes sense to me. The 5-Second Rule works. Apparently, our brains are wired to keep us alive and protect us from doing things that are scary, uncertain, uncomfortable, or difficult. I'm grateful to my brain for wanting to protect me but, in my opinion, doing that which is uncomfortable is what causes growth.

Case in point? Doing necessary strength training aka weight-bearing exercises. I may not like doing it but I sure like having done it. Making the decision to do it is in my control and it's my job to push myself.

I've strategically placed my dumbbells in our master bath vanity area where they are in full view in front of a large mirror. I look at the weights, then look myself in the eye and start the countdown: 5, 4, 3, 2... Oh hell. Pick them up and get it over with.

Yet another miracle. She can be taught.

LOOSE LEAF PAGES
Bonnie Watkins

Tiny threads of morning sun edge around the curtains
And wake me from sleep unwillingly.
Curling into a question mark, I flip over, covering my eyes
    with a fat pillow.
"Go away, Day. Not yet."

The day before brought uncertain medical reports,
Not yet devastating nor life-threatening,
Just annoying and expensive tests to come.
More body maintenance as I grow older but also add wisdom
    and experience.

Then, the evening brings a gathering of artists
To encourage, challenge, question, inspire.
The uncomfortable previous question of stopping art
Or even quitting altogether resurfaces.

Is that why I've been so long away from frequent writing?
As on the piano, do I need simply to return to daily Hanon
    finger exercises,
Short, imperfect, uncertain poems, rough and jagged all
    round,
Uncertain, unfinished, loose leaf pages, unbound,
    unfinished?

Here then…this uncertain offering…the first loose leaf page.

VERNIE

Shawn M. LaTorre

I always think of Vernie, a next-door neighbor lady, when I think back to forms of generosity in my youth. At first blink, she may not be the kind of lady you would expect to be so kind. She smoked cigarettes, drank when she felt like it, and had three beautiful children. Blackie, Vernie's husband, worked in the foundry in our industrial small town and came dragging home at five-thirty, dirty as anyone I'd ever seen, removed his shoes in the garage, climbed two small steps up to open the screen door to the kitchen and headed straight to the bathroom. Somehow in the quagmire of pretty tough economic times, Vernie found the time each summer to call all the kids in the neighborhood over to play Gin Rummy or some other penny game. She looked like a card shark, smoke encircling her head, glass of beer on the table, laughing at whatever came up. We had a blast munching on nuts, gingersnaps or pretzels, and drinking real soda–Coke usually–while we played. She'd often shoo us out before Blackie got home.

Vernie, like most moms in the area, hung her laundry out on the lines to dry. Seems like every day she had a batch of clothes and sheets drying out there. She and Blackie had a dog named Lassie that could smile. So, on top of the commands of shake, speak, lie down, we could ask Lassie to smile and she'd do it by baring lips back and showing all of her front teeth! I've only met one dog since then that smiles on command like that. One time Blackie was out back wearing a white muscle-tee shirt with some sort of blue work pants listening to Tiger baseball on a small radio. Clean clothes flapped on the line, and Lassie sauntered over to greet me before Blackie did. Must have been summer and must have been a weekend. That's just a snapshot of a sweet memory I still think about.

At holiday time, Vernie sent our family (probably others, too) the most incredible assortment of baked goods in a special oblong metal tin. She must have been baking and freezing all year, so varied were the cookies. Pecan balls, thin mint cookies, sugar cookies, brownies, layered chocolate chip bars, lemon bars, and more. Mom knew to put the tin up after we'd each had one, because we were like a pack of hungry wolves when something like that showed up and we could've devoured everything in no time if left to our own devices. Families in our neighborhood didn't have much, but we sure knew who to go to when Halloween came around. There, beneath her basement stairwell, were a couple of barrels chock-full of homemade clown costumes, wigs, old dresses, wings, kids overalls, and hats. I think she loved it when we needed to borrow things, since her kids were already grown and out of the house and these costume pieces surely carried bits of lingering happy memories just waiting to be released again.

When I came home from college for short breaks, I always tried to take time to walk over to say hi to Vernie. She'd come to open the door, laugh and say, "Come on in here girl! Sit down, and let me get you a glass of beer!" With that, she'd ask me about school, my classes, and fill me in on any neighborhood news. In so many ways, it seemed Vernie liked her life as much as she might have battled with it. She could dress up and look so fancy for weddings, showers, and parties. Even as she was aging, I caught glimpses of the younger woman she must have been, a couple of times when I glanced her way at these events. She began asking me to come over to help clean her house, which looked pretty spotless to me. She was a stickler for a clean floor though, so I had to get down on my hands and knees and scrub her floors—"HEY! Don't forget the corners!" Her arthritis wouldn't allow her to clean like she wanted to anymore and I know it bothered her. But it was summertime and I appreciated whatever money she paid. I can still hear her rolling, raspy laugh in my mind. She'd close her eyes, lean forward, and her shoulders would just shake with laughter. Sometimes she'd throw out a curse word here or there, when she came over to talk with our mom. "Jeezuz," she'd cackle. She's passed on now, but I think of her often, and wish every neighborhood with young kids could have at least one Vernie!

SHOOTING STARS

Margaret Dubay Mikus

Lying back on the dew-damp
cedar-plank picnic table
in the backyard in Harper Woods
probably sometime in the late sixties.

Summer. Night. Crickets.
Looking for shooting stars with Dad.
Don't remember if we saw any,
but still the smell and feel of wet wood,
exhilaration of adventure out in the dark.

Probably the Perseid meteor shower
in August I'd guess, like now. Cool last night.
Out for an hour and a half after midnight:
saw 3. No mosquitoes. Clear skies a while,
too much light. Tonight, warmer, mostly cloudy.
Five minutes: 1 mosquito. 0 shooting stars.

Watch clouds move, head tilted back on
wrought iron chair, neck propped by hood rolled down,
stars pop in and out of transient gaps.
Thinking back, like details of a movie playing,
remembering, connected to her back then,
connected to them.

In a few years I will leave home
with whatever I've learned about anything,
seeking expansion, liberation, to find who I am
in the age of upheaval, Vietnam War, assassination.
Rare would be these quiet moments of sharing again.

Young lack of understanding
how short number the days
how finite the opportunities
for the small things to build memories.
Do not know even now what turns out

to be important, what will stick to you like Velcro.

WHAT WENT UNSAID
Pat Anthony

after she sold the boarding house
and moved into the tiny apartment
was how she never had quite enough
left over from Grandpa's railroad pension
to buy ingredients for the cake-like hermits

she loved to bake just like those from
Wolferman's on Petticoat Lane in Kansas City
fat cookies rich in cinnamon and nutmeg
butter and brown sugar, plumped raisins
and English walnuts cut to a coarse chop

she favored my father and filled a tin
that traveled between them and when
it came back empty would tell him
with her lilting Irish laugh that there'd be
more when he brought her the ingredients

later, while filling her prescriptions
he'd go to the corner grocery, extract
the tattered list he kept in his billfold
and gather her favorite spices, sugar
throw in a bunch of perfect Tokay grapes

for when dusk cooled her tiny kitchenette
theirs a wordless understanding between a boy
raised by his grandmother in Oklahoma's red dust
and this Irish *Máthair chríona,* who knew
a tin of cookies feeds both stomach and heart.

ANTICIPATING A ZADIE
Marlene B. Samuels, Ph.D.

Did my advancing age transform me into a cynic or have I simply become a realist? The majority of my women friends—my contemporaries for sure, and their husbands—are grandparents or grandparents-in-waiting, my new term for them. Earlier this summer, at a barbecue, I mentioned that my older son, a mere child of thirty-four, just got engaged. Without exception, they cooed congratulations, each followed with comments intended to keep me from losing hope that one day in the not-too-distant future, I too would enjoy the rewards of being a grandparent.

It never occurred to me that I should worry about, or anticipate with great excitement, becoming a grandparent. Not long after my son told us he'd proposed to his long-time girlfriend, he and my husband and I were out to dinner. Between the soup and salad courses, my son probed, "So, would you two be upset if I didn't have kids?"

"Why would I be upset?" I asked, surprised. "If you don't want children, don't have them. Not my decision."

My husband appeared genuinely surprised by my answer, but sometimes is smart enough to know when to keep quiet. The next day, I shared our dinner conversation with a long-time woman friend, who herself happens to be a grandmother. She, too, expressed surprise. Am I a deficient aging mother of a grown man because I'm not interested in voicing my opinions regarding his decision not to have children? I want to believe that instead, it's because I had my own children ten years later than most of my friends had theirs and the delay afforded me time and opportunities to establish both independence and a professional life. When marriage and children did enter my scene, I was stunned by the degree of energy, time, emotional commitment, and sacrifice required to do a good job of it.

Yes, growing older has turned me into a bit of a cynic, but I've also evolved into a realist about parenting. Before I could restrain my mouth, I blurted out to my son, "I'll tell you to a certainty, having children and being a parent is not for the faint of heart, nor is it for the selfish." But the other part of my reaction to his announcement stems from my never having had grandparents—or rather, of course, I had them but never knew them. It was my son's announcement that evoked a significant memory about the concept of grandparents, what I came to refer to as my "Zadie Envy."

Each and every one of my grandparents had been murdered in Europe by Nazis during World War II. Add to it, that in my old Montreal neighborhood where I was growing up, two distinct populations made their home: Québécois French laborers, and immigrant Jewish Holocaust survivors from Europe, like my own family. They'd landed in Canada after their liberation from the camps. Generally, old Jews were rarely seen, and none of my friends had grandparents, either.

I was in a community devoid of grandparents so, consequently, had a limited understanding of the term "grandparents." Yet the mere idea of grandparents accounted for many of my great and youthful disappointments, really because of my friend Ruthie's Zadie. My sheltered life of limited exposure to the world outside of our shtetl-like St. Urbane neighborhood accounts for my convoluted beliefs.

Ruthie Whitefish was my best friend growing up. Better yet, we had more than our interests in common. Ruthie's family was a mirror image of my own. Her father was from Poland, like mine; her mother from Romania, like mine; and Ruthie's older brother, Issey—the same age as my older brother—had also been born in Germany in a D.P. Camp (displaced persons camp) just like mine. But one thing made Ruthie's family dramatically different from mine. Ruthie had a *Zadie* (grandfather). This highly pious, bearded, old Jewish man was the epitome of a "Zadie." To us children, the man appeared beyond ancient—like Moses incarnate—but in view of my current advancing age, I'm now positive that Zadie placed somewhere in the range of mid-sixties, seventy tops.

Ruthie adored Zadie. Her mother, Sylvia, catered to Zadie as much and often as possible. All the Whitefishes were thrilled to have the old man as a boarder in their flat, happier still that he was content and adored the children.

On weekdays, after Ruthie returned home from school, when Sylvia wasn't home yet from her Kosher bakery job, Zadie was sure to be there. Seconds after Ruthie walked in, she headed straight for the kitchen table, where Zadie could be found studying his Hebrew texts. And there, on the table across from Zadie, in the center of a bottle-green glass plate, sat a butter and raspberry jam sandwich, crusts removed, that he'd prepared. Next to the plate was a half-glass of milk.

On my lucky days, I'd be invited to go home with Ruthie, and it was on those very lucky days that Zadie placed two plates, two sandwiches, and two half-glasses of milk on the table. "Sailboats or boxes?" he'd ask Ruthie, hovering a long breadknife over the sandwich on one of the plates.

"Today, I want sailboats! Yesterday," she announced enthusiastically, "was boxes, remember Zadie?" Nodding, Zadie rested the knife atop the sandwich, cutting it in half on an angle, then in half again creating four triangle-shaped mini-sandwiches. Next, he'd turn his gaze to me, knife hovering above a sandwich once more.

"And you, *ziese kleine maydalah* (sweet little girl), also sailboats?"

"No, I like boxes." I was beyond ecstatic watching Zadie busy himself creating my butter and jam boxes. But I also was overcome by intense jealousy. Not only did Zadie make little snacks for my best friend, they played games together—checkers, tic-tac-toe, hangman—and they worked on Ruthie's math homework, too. Often, on Sundays, Zadie took Ruthie and Issey to matinee movies or downtown to feed the pigeons at St. Catherine's Square, or ducks in the pond at Mt. Royal park. There were swings and an ice cream shop at the top of Mt. Royal. More than anything, I wanted a Zadie of my very own. No longer did I care to ask for a pet. But a Zadie—an old man who'd live in our house—one who'd do all the things with me that Ruthie's Zadie did with her, that's what I wanted more than anything in the world.

Because all the parents in my neighborhood were Holocaust survivors, almost none of their parents had survived, so almost none of us had real grandparents. Montreal's Jewish Federation—in a program like foster care but for elderly who'd lost everyone—paid Jewish families stipends to provide the rare old Jewish survivor with room and board, in a home environment. Ruthie got her Zadie exactly this way. He arrived at the Whitefishes' home just about the time Ruthie began to walk.

One particular Sunday, Ruthie and Zadie were heading to the newly released "Lassie Come Home" movie. She hadn't invited me to join them. On that day I knew the time had come. I burst into my mother's workroom, shouting above the noise of her sewing machine. "Mom, mom, I have to talk to you! It's really important!"

"What is it? What's happened?" She shouted back, taking her feet off the machine's heavy pedal.

"Mom, you know that Ruthie has a Zadie, right?"

"Of course I know."

"Well, why can't we get one? Can't we look for a Zadie to live with us and to do all those things with me that Zadie Whitefish does with Ruthie? He could live in the extra room by the kitchen!"

My mom was rendered speechless. I truly believed that Zadies (Bubbies, too) were simply religious old Jews who lived in an extra room in the house, did fun things with the children, and had piles of books all in Hebrew. I waited for my mother's response, one that didn't come too readily. "Mom, did you hear what I said?"

"Let me talk to daddy about this. We'll see." My mother whispered, staring out the workroom window onto our street. But I never did see.

CAMP TEE ATA
Lois Ann Bull

My mother and I had a very strong bond. I loved her, and I knew she loved me. In 1948, we challenged the bond and tested its strength.

I was seven. My brother, one year older, loved sleepover summer camp and spent the whole winter talking about it. Not to be outdone, I asked to go to Camp Tee Ata as a Brownie Scout, also a sleepover camp. Barbara Smith, the teenager next door worked there as a counselor.

Wanting to go with all my heart, I put on a campaign worthy of a presidential candidate to get permission. I wore my mother down. Against her better judgment, she signed the permission papers. Forty dollars for a two-week period was a bargain price, and she hoped I would enjoy it as much as I thought I would. Besides, two weeks didn't seem too long. The week prior, I packed and repacked my trunk daily, as I envisioned the wonderful time waiting for me. Excitement controlled my life, and true to form, I became so overstimulated, I suffered through a terrible migraine headache the day before I left.

On opening Sunday, my parents drove me to the Bear Mountain campsite. They helped me unpack and make my bed before we walked the grounds. I thought the latrines smelled terrible, but the mess hall looked nice, and the smell of cinnamon greeted us as we passed the kitchen.

After our tour, my parents collected their belongings in preparation for their departure. Then reality hit me. My parents were leaving. I could barely catch my breath.

"I don't want to stay," I blurted out frantically. "I want to go home with you."

My father looked shocked. My mother became undone. No doubt she felt no more ready to leave me than I her. But her upper lip didn't quiver the way mine did.

The counselor hovered nearby. She stepped right up and gently grasped my hand. "You'll have a wonderful time here," she said to me as she gently separated me from my parents. She continued, "We'll get ready for your swimming tryouts," motioning to my parents with her head, I suppose, to get a move on.

"No," I yelled. "I want to go home with my mommy and daddy."

The counselor thought she knew better and reassured my parents that I would be fine.

"Are you sure?" my mother asked, and I knew it would be a big mistake. I sniffled and leaked tears between big gulps of air.

"Oh yes," said the counselor. "This reaction never lasts long. She's a big girl, and she'll get interested as soon as you leave." Deciding to agree with the counselor for want of a suitable alternative, they said "goodbye" and walked toward the car park. As they left, my sobs became louder. The flow of tears resembled a river. I collapsed on my cot in a weeping heap. The wonderful woolen blanket from home pricked my cheek. The other Brownie Scouts in the tent looked at me as if they, too, questioned the wisdom of being at camp.

We put on our swimsuits and went to the waterfront for the tryouts. Blinded by my tears, I tripped on the small rocks on the dirt path, but the counselor clutched my hand, preventing me from falling, or maybe from running after my parent's car. I continued to cry.

Standing on the dock waiting my turn, I felt wet, cold, and miserable. Thinking about my parents, I began to shake as tears streamed down my cheeks. The Waterfront Director told my counselor to take me back to my tent until I'd recovered. "There's enough water in this lake without her adding to it," she said, and the teenager led me away.

I cried for three days. At every opportunity, usually rest hour and after dinner, I wrote letters home, writing about my misery and promising that if they would fetch me, I would do dishes for a year. In block printing that deteriorated into illegible strokes and lines as emotion overcame me, I begged and promised until, so worked up, I'd have to quit.

In one letter, I told my mother I would buy her a mink coat if I could come home. Anything they asked I would do if only they would rescue me. All the persuasive techniques I had used to get permission to attend camp I used in reverse. By Tuesday, the eye flashes of aura began signaling a terrible migraine headache. I spent the day in the infirmary where the nurse put me to bed with aspirin, and I slept until the next day.

On Wednesday, the fourth day, Gladys Smith, our "busy-body" next-door neighbor arrived with a few forgotten items for her daughter, Barbara. Mrs. Smith stopped by to see me, but a face from home made me feel worse. After she left, I laid on my camp bed, inconsolable, much to the worry of my counselor and the other Brownies. Many of them felt homesick now that the newness had worn off and a few joined me in hysterics.

That evening just before dinner, I had to report to the Camp Director's office. Not knowing the reason for the summons, I worried the whole way that I might be punished for wanting to leave. The Camp Director, Miss Dora, a most un-motherly woman, awaited me. She asked if the treatment I'd received at the camp had been unfair or too harsh? I nodded no. But when asked why the tears, I said, "Because I want my mommy. I want to go home."

She asked if I'd like to phone home. I brightened. I had no idea the camp had a telephone. I think the Camp Director hoped my mother would tell me to shape up and act like a true Brownie Scout.

Once the line began to ring, she handed me the phone. Mother answered. The sound of her voice undid me. A fresh batch of tears cascaded, and my words dissolved into blubbering. I never gave my mother a chance to say anything beyond the initial "Hello." Not wanting to lose a minute, I started begging her to come for me.

Two of my distress letters, scribbled and tear stained, had arrived in the mail. The error in Mom's judgment had been revealed. Some seven-year-olds might be ready for sleep-away camp, but not her daughter.

Whether it was the promise of the mink coat or dish duty for a year, I'll never know. But she couldn't bear my pain and wanted me home as soon as possible.

The next morning, she arrived right after breakfast. Miss Dora's disapproving gaze didn't bother Mother at all. She packed up my foot-locker, and as we walked to the car in front of the teens lassoed into helping us, I clutched Mom's hand with a white-knuckled grip.

It would be six years before I grew up enough to try camp again.

THE SWOOPER

Rollyn Carlson

Who else but Lynda could have talked us into believing that the back of her neighbor's house sat on top of a long-smoldering volcano, and it was coincidentally scheduled to erupt at the exact same time that we were sitting there? Who else could have talked us into believing we could transport ourselves to magical universes simply by building tents out of blankets we found in the bottom of Neena's front closet? She was made for the stage, but the cosmos had other plans for her.

Her biggest moment in the spotlight occurred when she was about ten years old and made the front page of Austin's newspaper. At this time, the paper was delivered twice a day. The morning paper was the *Austin-American*; the evening paper was the *Statesman*. In kid world, we viewed the two newspapers in this way: the morning paper contained the fluff—things like Dear Abby, Heloise's Housekeeping Tips, and Peanuts. The truly grown-up stuff was found in the evening paper, the paper that our parents read while sitting on the couch in the living room, shaking their head and muttering "Mmm Mmm Mmm," while they took in the terrible state of affairs.

But I digress. The riveting point of this tale is that Lynda, at her tender age, made the front page of the *Austin Statesman*, the evening paper, the *intellectual* food of grown-ups. And she did it, as usual, with all the drama she could muster.

It happened in the late spring and during the week, which means my sister and I were stuck in San Antonio, in compulsory punishment for children otherwise known as school, when the event happened. By the time we were able to hear the full story, Lynda had sailed through the stormy seas of the event's horror and made it to the tranquil waters of celebrity *du jour*. We had heard about the incident with *"the swooper"* and were chomping at the bit to get to Austin to hear the entire story.

According to our heroine, it was a cool spring evening. Homework and dinner were finished, and rather than retire to her room, she headed down the street to the house of two other members of the notorious neighborhood Gang, Mimi and Jan, who were apparently given strict instructions not to leave the yard since it was getting dark. The Gang leader and her followers opted for sticking to the Waters' side yard, which had a heavy wooden picnic table situated right next to a large oak tree. I wasn't there so I'm only guessing, but I suspect it didn't take long for Lynda to launch into a story that required her to use the picnic table as a stage. It was perfect because their house had a floodlight attached to the roof, and that would serve as stage lighting.

By the time I was able to hear the details firsthand, Mimi and Jan told me they couldn't recall actually seeing *the swooper*. All they remembered was that it was dark, Lynda was standing on the table telling a story that required large "gestations" with her arms, and then…came the screams. They didn't even remember the plot. What they did remember was she was coming to an important part, and she was standing up, her back to the tree, waving her arms.

Suddenly, Lynda felt something hit her head. She didn't have time to throw her arms over her head to protect herself. She recalled hearing a *"swooshing"* sound and then came the next hit, but this time it came with what felt like claws—long, sharp claws—being dragged across the top of her head and her forehead. She began to scream and ducked down to a squat. She threw her arms over her head, but whatever it was would not let her off that easy. Mimi and Jan sat frozen on the grass. Lynda continued to scream, and flailed with her arms against the dark assailant. Her screams brought Mimi and Jan's parents out of the house, not to mention every other neighbor. Whatever it was was gone, but when Lynda took her hands away from her head, both hands, as well as her face, were covered in blood.

The Austin Police Department had probably been having a quiet night when the call from Mrs. Waters came in and set off a chain of events. The fire department was monitoring the emergency system radio and got into the act. A tenacious reporter for the *Austin Statesman* was also monitoring emergency calls. Within three minutes, the sirens could be heard screaming through the streets, and flashing lights were streaming across the picture windows of every house in the neighborhood.

The reporter was probably sure that this story would get him a *Pulitzer,* which in turn would get him out of Texas and on to the giddy heights of the *New York Times.* Instead, he found that he had to piece a story together from three terrified kids, still standing in the dark in front of the entire neighborhood, who had now spilled out from their houses into their front yards. But he was undaunted. He had his trusty camera and lined Lynda and her two cohorts against the house and took a picture that would be splashed across the next day's paper. Luck was with him; the story was getting better. This was Texas after all, so here came the instantly-formed neighborhood militia—men standing tensely in their front yards with their hunting rifles, without a clue as to what they were hunting. All sorts of theories were being shouted out. It could have been a giant bat, larger than anything ever seen, with claws, and harboring disease. It could be a wild mammal that had retreated up into the highest parts of the tree, never mind that they couldn't come up with a reasonable explanation to account for the swooshing sound. Talks of nightly neighborhood patrols were being discussed.

Now the reporter decided to take several additional pictures of Lynda solo, with extra care to show the deep claw marks. Lynda made sure her eyes were as wide as possible, something she excelled at. She was reveling in the attention, until she heard several of the adults discussing rabies shots, and heard her mother saying she would be calling the pediatrician first thing the next morning. All the kids sucked their breath in. That meant shots…in her stomach…with a needle that, swear to god, was 12 inches long…for days…which was the same thing as forever.

Lynda was led home. The swirling lights on top of the police car and fire truck were turned off. The neighbors slowly dispersed to their respective homes. The neighborhood slowly descended into darkness. Lynda's picture would show up the next day on the front page of the *Statesman*; her encounter with an unknown flying being with claws made headlines. Neighbors made good their threat to walk up and down Winstead Lane in the dark with their rifles, mostly posing as a threat to innocent dogs, cats, and raccoons, who had the good sense to lay low for several nights. It was all pretty heady stuff.

The Great Horned Owl in the Waters' giant oak tree settled down comfortably in her nest with her recently hatched owlets. She tolerated the humans running around her home during the day. She would even tolerate them walking around the yard in the evening. But when the human stood too close to her tree to suit her, and climbed up too close to her nest, and waved her arms in what was surely a sign of attack, that was simply the last straw for the protective mother. She made several dives, one with her talons out to make sure her intentions were understood. She was as surprised as the humans at the noise that young human could make.

I want to believe the owlets made it to adulthood with Mother Owl standing guard. If so, without a single word of thanks from the neighborhood vigilantes, rodents in the neighborhood were kept at bay. Lynda would retain bragging rights that would spread beyond the neighborhood, at least until Fall.

B+

Jane Gragg Lewis

My eyes cannot believe what they see. A measly B+? Is she kidding me? Now I hate Mrs. Thompson, my second grade teacher, even more.

She has put all the drawings on the bulletin board and mine is in the middle where everyone is sure to see that I'm the only one who didn't get an A. My drawing is so much better than all the rest. It's a picture of a horse behind a fence in a pasture. I'd like to see her try to draw a horse *behind* a fence. He's standing under an apple tree with a smile on his face. It's obvious it's an apple tree 'cause I put lots of perfectly shaped, shiny red apples on it. I even put some on the ground. Definitely A work. I want to say A+ work, but pride goeth before a fall—or so Reverend Long is always saying.

And look! Everyone else drew the same thing. They all drew pictures of their families. Let's face it. If Fred got an A for that lousy mess, I really should have an A+.

I'm still fuming on the way to my bus after school, and I complain to Gloria. She gives me a funny look and tells me, "But the assignment was 'draw a picture of your family.'"

It was? Well, whatever. Mrs. Thompson is still the meanest teacher at Berryhill School.

And I just can't seem to let this go. Thinking about it is nibbling away at all my time. Daddy's been in Baltimore all week, so on Friday, my newest complaint about Mrs. Thompson is sitting right beside me on the steps of the side porch, waiting for him to get home from the airport. As soon as he drives up, I'm waiting at his car door before he even has a chance to open it.

My words stumble over each other as I tell him my sad story.

"This happened Tuesday, and you're *still* this mad at Mrs. Thompson about it?" he asks.

"Of course!"

"You didn't follow directions, Jane. How *could* she give you an A?"

Is he seriously on her side? He knows how horrible she is. I can't believe it! I waited all week to hear *this*?

"Look at it this way," he says. "You didn't follow directions and you still got a B+. Just a tiny bit below an A. She *could* have given you an F."

I frown at him, trying to figure out where *my* daddy went. Who stole him out of his body? Things like that can really happen, you know, and Mrs. Thompson probably has something to do with it.

Then he adds, "Listen, you like your picture. I'm sure I will, too. Who cares if that mean old witch likes it or not? What does *she* know about art?"

Whew! Now *that* sounds more like my daddy!

"Let it go. It's not worth wasting your time."

"Okay. I will, Daddy," I tell him, hugging his arm as we go inside.

But I know I'll *never* let it go. I'll never forget this B+ and I'll still hate Mrs. Thompson and be mad about it even when I'm really, *really* old.

VENTRILOQUIST FOR JESUS
Claire Butler

I'm sorry I didn't just say the words.

In the summer of 1968, I was thirteen and headed to my very first summer camp – a church camp located in the foothills of the Great Smoky Mountains in Sevierville, Tennessee. Two of my friends from church, Joanne and Sue, were to be my cabin mates for one whole week for what I imagined would be the time of my life. I had always wanted to go to camp as my best friend had attended camp for years, and I had saved all of her postcards from camp to read over and over as she described meeting new friends, sleeping in cabins, and canoeing.

Our days began at daybreak, when eighty boys and girls met in the Great Hall for breakfast and prayers. Meals were served country style at great, long tables, where we passed steaming bowls of scrambled eggs, grits, bacon, biscuits and country sausage gravy. We were each assigned daily chores such as kitchen duty, clean-up, or latrine-scrubbing. Our daily routine included swimming, volleyball, meals, scripture study, and evening lectures in the Great Hall.

One morning we were told that a well-known, evangelistic ventriloquist and his wooden doll would make an appearance after dinner that evening. Upon hearing that news, the girls were giddy and the boys pretended to throw their voices. The only time I had ever seen a ventriloquist was on the Ed Sullivan Show with Edgar Bergen and his Charlie McCarthy doll. I knew there had to be an obvious trick for a person to throw his voice, and being the curious sort that I was, I was early for a front row seat. I was determined to learn the secret.

That night Joanne sat to my right and Sue to my left, and we were dead center in the front row. The ventriloquist was already seated on stage with his doll on his lap. The doll was turning its head back and forth, rolling its eyes and opening and closing its mouth while everyone took their seats. I could feel the excitement welling up inside of me and my seatmates. Suddenly, the doll yelled out its name and introduced the ventriloquist as his "dummy friend." Everyone clapped and laughed, and some of the boys whistled!

I paid way more attention to watching the ventriloquist's mouth than to watching the doll. After a few minutes, I realized that this doll's friend must truly have been throwing his voice, as impossible as it seemed. I could not see his mouth move at all. I leaned into Sue's ear and whispered, "This guy is really good." And just that fast, the doll directed its attention to me and said accusingly, "What did you say, little girl?"

I froze. With over eighty pairs of eyes staring at me, with a flush of embarrassment, and with fear of retribution I sat mute, just like the doll when not being manipulated by its friend. The doll asked me again, but louder, "What did you say, little girl?" My vocal cords refused to cooperate, but somehow with considerable effort I managed to say the word "nothing." The ventriloquist stood up from his stool, walked to the edge of the stage and pointed his finger at me. What happened next caused me post-traumatic distress for years after. For the rest of my teenage years, whenever I saw a ventriloquist's doll, I would relive the entire episode – the flushing, the inability to speak, and the frightful accusation that I was a liar.

Yes, a liar. Right there in front of over eighty people, this man and his doll labeled me a liar, and asked me if I knew that was the Devil's work? Did I even know why I was at this camp? I could not speak, I could not cry, I could not run because I was frozen to my folding chair. Even the heat of all those eyes staring at me was not enough to thaw me from that chair, because I didn't know what they were thinking. The room was awash in hushed voices and the ventriloquist's piercing eyes bore holes through me.

I stole a side-glance at Sue, who had turned paler than her already pale complexion. I was sure she was thinking that the next thing that would happen was that the ventriloquist would ask her what I had said. Surely she was embarrassed to be sitting next to me. I braced myself for his next question when, without further humiliation, he returned to his seat and began witnessing for Jesus.

Years later, I picked up a memoir aptly titled "Knock Wood," by Candice Bergen, the only child of ventriloquist Edgar Bergen. Growing up, Candice was routinely referred to as "Charlie McCarthy's little sister," a reference she grew to resent because Charlie presented powerful competition for her father's attention. She described her incredibly sad childhood as taking second place in her father's life behind his wooden dolls. He often carried Charlie around with him and conversed with and chastised Candice through him, which greatly confused her as a child. I had a sense of what she felt.

While reading her story, I thought about that awful event so long ago in the foothills of the Great Smoky Mountains and the ventriloquist talking through his doll about his dedication to Jesus. I wondered if that man ever gave a second thought about humiliating a thirteen-year-old girl in front of what seemed like a thousand people to her. I wondered if he really wanted to spread the love and kindness of Jesus – or was that just part of the show?

I'm sorry I didn't speak up. I'm sorry because if I had told what I had really said then maybe he would have been the one to be embarrassed that night. As I grew older, like Candice, I found my voice again, and learned, like Candice, that preserving one's dignity, even if it means publicly standing up for yourself, is better than allowing someone to steal your voice. It's better to knock wood.

MEMORIALIZING AUNTIE MAGGIE
Debra Dolan

"And now here is my secret, a very simple secret:
It is only with the heart that one can see rightly;
what is essential is invisible to the eye."

— *The Little Prince*, Antoine de Saint-Exupery

She came into my life when I was desperate for comfort, protection, and love. I felt very much alone. There was no one to express my feelings to and, at 11 years, I lacked the words to describe my experience. Although I have aged, she has not. I am now older than she has ever been and although I understand it is rare for this kind of interpersonal relationship to remain in adulthood, I don't remember a day without my imaginary friend.

Auntie Maggie has been very much alive in my mind and heart; a confidant, a security in times of loneliness and uncertainty, a beautiful woman who has led an interesting life. This woman has loved me 'to the moon and back.' I talk to her often, keeping her alive in my simple and uncomplicated West Coast world. I love her. I don't know how to say goodbye. The lie to others of her "real and true" existence has recently become a burden as I sift through documents of ancestry and construct a memoir. Perhaps her ongoing presence in my life will say more about me than I want anyone to know. Even today, I still want to make her proud and preserve the meaning she brought to young Debbie's life.

When I was young, I used to take the train to Montreal alone to spend a day with my auntie. I used my summer babysitting money: five dollars per day for caring for three children. She always treated me special. Routinely, we would go out-to-lunch, a diner near her home, shop on Rue Saint-Catherine, and view a matinee at Loews Theatre. She was often accompanied by a different man on these visits—all tall, handsome, intelligent, brooding. I believe they paid the bills. Auntie

Maggie was beautiful and fun, with an infectious lovely smile and deep raspy laugh. I remember her smoking. She was the 'keeper' of all my secrets, listening intently and asking a lot of questions with keen interest. She never married or had children, living life on her own terms. She was a voracious reader and her private space was dominated by books.

I tried to erase her from my mind when I went to university, sensing she was no longer necessary. She fought valiantly. Although I never wanted it to be violent, in my mind she died of suicide, alone, in a rooming house on Rue Saint-Antoine. She had taken many pills and was found lying on the floor, bottle of whiskey by her hand. No note, no last despairing phone message. It seemed fitting for a woman on her own at that time perishing in this way. I was greatly influenced by all the authors I was reading: Anaïs Nin, Virginia Woolf, Sylvia Plath, Daphne de Maurier, Rosamunde Pilcher. I remember her crying, often. Auntie Maggie had a view of the St. Lawrence River, which she said connected us—Montreal Quebec to Cornwall Ontario, two hours away. I reminisce that she always looked rather bohemian, free-spirited, fun-loving and unconventional. Her purses were small and her lipstick was red. She had stunning thick brunette hair.

My mother, her younger sister, did not like or approve of her. She was watchful of our time together in Montreal and my storytelling, and never let me stay the night. I always had to have a same-day return train ticket or I was not allowed to go. In 1974, there was a terrible snowstorm and my stepfather drove all the way to Montreal, in dreadful conditions, to retrieve me as the trains had stopped operating. He was very angry and my mother said Maggie "remained reckless." There were angry words. I was grounded 'til spring.

Everything I did or said was magic to Auntie Maggie. She has always been very real for me, even now, although my rational mind knows that she has never existed. When I think of her, I feel loved and happy and light of burden. I see her very clearly in my mind, especially during the 1960s-'70s. Thinking about my special relationship with her brings me joy, as it remains immensely important still and I suspect always will be. How can someone not always love another who delighted in your company, was always happy to see you, and gave you undivided attention? There has never been another like her.

All my life I have been told, almost in a negative or suspicious way, that I have a vivid and overactive internal life. I suspect, on reflection,

I have used these visions and character creations as a tool to control anxiety and relax. For many years, I wondered if I was crazy or abnormal, related to connecting with Auntie Maggie regularly in my adulthood, when alone, knowing I had attempted to knock her off in my teens. Or has it just been wonderful having a forever friend to engage with when necessary?

I don't know if I will ever be able to let her go.

LOST CHILDHOOD

Lois Ann Bull

Sulking in the TV room because I was fifteen and had no plans to be out that Saturday evening, I heard my father shout. It took me a moment to realize he'd bellowed my name. Because my father never yelled at me, I was shocked and disoriented. I lowered the TV volume and opened the door.

"Did you want me?" I called, unsure which way to direct my voice.

"Get your mother," he barked with an urgency that kept me from asking questions.

None of his usual polite "Sweetheart, would you please, or thank you," accompanied the demand. From where I stood in the hall, I noticed his feet resting on top of his bedspread. I couldn't see any more of him, but decided he must be lying down. Hurrying downstairs, I called to my mother to come. Then, so stricken by my father's odd, seemingly angry tone, I turned off the television and went to my bedroom again, shutting the door. Without lights, I sat on my bed fully dressed and stared out the window, wallowing in teenage loneliness, self-pity, and self-imposed exile. High school and adulthood, long sought by me, began to tarnish.

The sound of a siren in the distance, wailing its warning, interrupted my despair. At first I ignored it, but as the sound increased, it forced me to listen. Each keen grew clearer and then louder. Some sixth sense told me it would come to my house. The insistent wailing acted like a demand, and I hoped it would go by, trying to kid myself into believing that it was not destined for us.

But it was, and once next to the house, its last voluminous shriek slowly shrank away, dragging my juvenile depression with it. The revolving red light, flickering at my periphery, bloodied the trees in our peaceful yard, its portent ominous. With the siren now devoid of sound, the silence was frightening.

Then I heard voices of strange men on our stairs and feet moving quickly. I remained hidden, scared, unmoving. The men went into the master bedroom and then, minutes later, out again, this time slowly. Images played out in my mind. I saw my father on that stretcher. I had no need to open the door to look. I knew. Words of caution floated to me, "careful, watch your step, ease to the right, careful of the balustrade," punctuated with heavy breathing, painting a picture for me of the difficulties of maneuvering their heavy burden down the curved staircase. Silence again. The yard, still flooded in blood red, remained motionless, as if standing guard in my stead while I furtively remained in darkness.

Then the wail cut into the stillness, as the ambulance hurried off. The sound faded into the night along with my father, eventually sounding more like a desperate cry as it distanced itself from me. Silence returned.

The view from my window remained unchanged. The yard appeared as peaceful as it had for fifteen years. The street light at the end of our property burned as always, still a beacon into my room during the tired night. Everything outside remained as it always had been. Inside things had changed. My earlier self-pity and discontent were forgotten with the enormity of the current event. What illness befell my father? Would he die? Would I ever see him again? How would my mother manage? Feeling sure she had gone with him, I realized it would be morning before I knew and maybe that would be better.

Overwhelmed, I undressed slowly, movements lead-like from grown-up concerns. I climbed into bed. My tense body, rigid from fear, gave way slowly to the familiar contours of the mattress. Finally, I relaxed into the pillow. Then hot tears began to seep. At first, one at a time, oozing out the corners of my eyes, burning my face, wetting the pillow, slowly building until overcome with anguish, I let them flow freely. I cried for my father and his pain, for my mother and her distress, and for myself and the childhood that leaked away like the sound of the ambulance, further and further into the dark night, until it was beyond my reach and gone forever.

WHY I DIDN'T BECOME A YOUNG WRITER

Deborah L. Bean

I've always had stories in my head. Love stories, murders, extra-terrestrial locations, conflict, struggle, and hope. It's how I put myself to sleep when all the day-to-day activities were overwhelming me. When I was working a full-time job, a part-time job, and going to school part-time while raising two small children. When I was working three part-time jobs, while going to school full-time and raising two children. And also, when I married and was only working one job while continuing to go to school, while raising teenagers. The stories have always been there.

After I married, I would tell my husband the ideas I came up with. I guess he got tired of hearing them, because he suggested that I write them down, which I started doing. Then, I finally got the courage to let a few other writers read my words and I was told I had some talent. One published author actually told me I had a "great voice."

Why didn't someone tell me this earlier? I'm specifically thinking of a ninth grade English teacher, when I was a student at Brazoswood High School in Lake Jackson, TX. Why didn't she say something back then? It might have changed my path.

We had an assignment. The story is that little Johnny tells his parents that his friend, who no one else has seen, broke the lamp. Johnny is sent to his room. Our task was to write the ending of the story, at least one paragraph.

It was a simple project for most of the class. We all were required to read our ending to the story—out loud. All the students in the class wrote and read a few sentences of how little Johnny was sorry for telling a lie, was punished, was forgiven, or some other generic, vanilla ending —but not me.

There was only one little problem. Because my last name is Bean, I was called on first. I'd worked really hard on the ending to that story. I told how, in Johnny's bedroom, there was an interdimensional portal. Johnny's "imaginary" friend was real. It took me four-and-a-half pages to finish that tale. Johnny's friend was the general of an invading army.

He told Johnny how he would bring his armies across the void and, together, they would conquer the Earth. At this point, little Johnny asks the general what conquer means. The story closed with the invader's answer. "Uh—it means help."

I was so happy at the imaginative ending I'd made of the assignment. Then, after I read it, every other student told their little moral ending in one-tenth the words I'd spoken. As more and more students finished the story, I felt more and more humiliated and embarrassed as teenagers often are. For decades, I thought I'd gotten the project wrong.

Of course I got an A. But my teacher never said one word about my submission. She never spoke of me having a good imagination and creating an imaginative ending that went far beyond what others had created. I was never encouraged to consider a writing career. Not. One. Word.

Was it because my story was so definitely genre fiction? Back then, in 1969, science fiction wasn't respected as it is these days, after four Star Trek series, plus all the movies; after the success of the Star Wars franchise; and even considering the Harry Potter books and movies, the Twilight books and movies, and all the other speculative fiction that surrounds us these days. Heck, even my mother enjoys urban fantasy now.

But back then, when I was considered a nerd, it wasn't with the respect the title brings today. So, even with a great grade, I still thought something was wrong with me. This brings me to the circumstances that made me believe I could be a writer someday.

In 2014, I received an email from Arizona State University. I still have no idea why I received it—what list they got my name from or anyone who could have suggested me. It told me about a program called **Your Novel Year**, where aspiring authors could be taught while they worked on a book project. All I had to do was write an essay of why I wanted to be in the program and include a sample chapter of my writing. And, best of all, it was targeted to sci-fi and fantasy.

So I entered.

Some months later I received a phone call telling me I'd been accepted. I screamed and shouted for joy when I heard. My husband came running, thinking I'd been hurt or something. I was one of only fourteen people who had been accepted—worldwide!

I finished that eighteen-month program and wrote that novel. I learned how to write much better than I ever had before. I learned tips and tricks to keep a story going, building tension into scenes, and all the little things that add up to the story—like weather, a character's emotions, colorful second characters, and making circumstances worse for my characters. Then I was taught how and when to edit. My book was edited and reviewed by several published authors who gave me more feedback.

That book, *The Moabim Atrocity*, was good for a starter novel but hasn't been published. Now I've started on something different, a YA series. Plus I've won a contest for a flash fiction story called *The Visiting Professor*, with a cash prize, and been published in the *Story Circle Journal*.

I can now call myself a writer.

As for that English teacher, hopefully she didn't short-circuit too many careers before their time. I think of all I could have accomplished if I'd kept writing back then. Instead, I'm beginning a new career at sixty, not fourteen. But at sixty, I have a lot more life experience to invest in my stories—more pain, more love, better judgment, and less fear. All I have to do now is keep trying and keep writing.

SPOTLIGHT ON PAT BEAN
by Susan Schoch

I am turning the tables here on Story Circle Network's accomplished interviewer, Pat Bean, to ask her a few questions. A retired journalist, Pat contributes substantially to SCN's publications, is active on the Board and on the Story Circle Book Reviews website. She also moderates SCN's online group, Writer2Writer. The author of a compelling book, *Travels with Maggie*, Pat is an adventurous woman who loves traveling, nature, reading, birding, painting with watercolors, her canine companion Scamp, and writing. She is always full of questions, usually ones that can't be answered, and always looking for a silver lining. Pat is blessed to be the mother of five, grandmother of 15, and great-grandmother of seven. Oh yes, she has some stories! Samples of her skillful and engaging writing follow this. I know you will enjoy meeting Pat here, and on her blog at https://patbean.net.

Will you tell us a little about your personal journey, Pat, and how you came to be a writer and a journalist?

I was a quite-young mother of four children, with a fifth soon to come, and my motherness was stretched to the moon and back. On this particular day, I found my oldest son teaching his siblings how to climb the backyard fence, while the youngest son had gotten into the sugar bowl, spreading sticky white granules all over the house, which sat in the middle of cockroach country. It went downhill from there.

When I was frazzled, to the point of feeling like a cockroach myself, my four-year-old son, Lewis, handed me a stemless yellow flower – which he had picked from the neighbor's yard and which I would hear about later. But the look of love on his grimy little face made everything that happened that day pale in comparison. Later that night, at about 1 a.m., I couldn't sleep until I got up and wrote a crude poem that I called "The Little Yellow Flower." It was the first time I had ever written anything that wasn't a list, a letter, or a school assignment, but from that second on, writing became as important to me as breathing.

For the next couple of years, I read lots of books about writing. But as a high school dropout, I didn't tell anyone that I want to be a writer. In my mind, writers were all well-educated, highly intelligent people – and then there was me. But when my oldest child was nine and my youngest two years old, I came across an ad for a reporter at the local newspaper, *The Brazosport Facts*, a 12,000-circulation daily.

Reporters write, I thought. I'm not sure where I got the balls but I applied for the reporting job. I lied on the application, saying I had a high school diploma. I admitted I had no experience, but balanced that by emphasizing that I was a fast learner. That was the truth. I had been a straight A student before I dropped out of high school.

Of course, I didn't get the job. A guy fresh out of college got it. I was bummed because the second I had walked into the paper's newsroom, I truly felt at home for the first time in my life. Not long afterwards, however, the paper's managing editor called and asked if I was interested in being a darkroom technician, an easy job for someone who is a fast learner, he said. I assumed he was looking at my application as we talked. I asked if I could write, too, and he said if I had time after my dark room duties.

I said yes – and five months later, I was promoted to reporter. Soon after, I sneaked into college, based on my ACT scores. I continued taking college classes, one a semester, right up until I retired. But I considered the four years I spent at The Facts better than any college education. No one had time to teach me how to do things at the paper – until I made a mistake. Then everyone had oodles of times to tell me how to do it right. I made lots of mistakes, but rarely the same one twice.

What led you to your nine-years-long adventure with your canine buddy, Maggie? What did you learn in the process of turning that experience into a memoir?

When I was about 10, I read *I Married Adventure* by Osa Johnson, and knew I wanted adventure in my life. When I read *Blue Highways* by William Least Heat Moon, I knew I wanted to travel full time across this beautiful country like he did in his van. By the time I got around to doing it, the van had become a 21-foot class C motorhome, which I named Gypsy Lee. Gypsy for my own wanderlust, and Lee after my grandfather Charles Forest Lee, from whom my mother said I inherited that wanderlust. Lee was also my mother's maiden name, and my middle name. I was 65 when I began what would become a nine-year-journey with only my dog Maggie as my companion. The adventure fulfilled one of my two lifetime dreams.

The second dream was to write a book, and the first two drafts of *Travels with Maggie* were written while I was on the road. I submitted the first draft to a Mayborn Non-Fiction Workshop, and it was chosen as one of the top ten entries, which earned me the right to a critique session with the other nine winners. My book got high marks from everyone – with one major exception. It lacked voice. I had written the book trying to hide that I was an old broad because I thought readers wouldn't be interested in anything that someone my age would have to say.

How did you find your way to Story Circle Network, and how has your involvement affected you and your writing?

It was 2010, in the middle of my RV-ing years, and I was in Texas when I saw an ad in *Writer's Digest* about a Story Circle Workshop. I attended and immediately knew this was the group I belonged in. No other writing group has given me such wholehearted support. Story Circle helped me find my voice, and finally – after 10 long years of trying to get it perfect – pushed me to finally self-publish my book. Everyone encouraged me, but the final push was from Story Circle member Sherry Wachter, who designed the cover and formatted the book. I can't thank Story Circle or Sherry enough, for helping me achieve the second of my life-long dreams.

How have your other passions – such as painting, birding, dogs, reading – shaped your life and your career as a writer?

Some people, and a tiny part of me envies them, can focus on one goal. They can accomplish great things. That's not me. I'm always afraid I'm going to miss something; I actually have a button that says: I Want it All!

As a journalist, I acted in local theater productions, hiked, took college classes, skied, white-water rafted, took up birding, and piddled with painting, which I do more of these days. But please don't call me an artist because I'm a writer, and the pressure to be good at writing is all my poor soul can handle.

I think all the things I do make me a better writer, but it means that I will never be one who can turn out a book in a year. I'm working now on my memoir, a book I'm tentatively calling Between Wars.

I began my journalism career in 1967 at the height of the Vietnam War. The first significant story with my byline on it in the newspaper was one in which I interviewed a mother whose son had been killed in that war.

I retired in 2004, the year we went back into Iraq a second time. I wrote several columns against that action. The book will follow my 37-year journalism career, along with the chaos that was often my home life during the early days. It takes me from being a high school dropout to associate editor of a 65,000-circulation daily newspaper.

Writing this book will take a massive amount of hard work. I'm expecting Story Circle to help me find the way to do it, and keep me on track. My heart frequently thanks our founder, Susan Wittig Albert, for creating this wonderful circle of writing women.

THE LITTLE GIRL IN THE PHOTOGRAPH
Pat Bean

I was in my 70s when a cousin sent me a small, black-and-white photo that changed the whole context of my childhood. I knew the picture was of me only because of its back inscription: Patricia Lee Joseph, age 3.

The little girl's pale, straw-colored hair was curled into neatly arranged ringlets, the puffed-sleeve, short frock she wore had clearly been starched and pressed to perfection and beneath her black patent-leather Mary Janes, she wore lace-trimmed socks.

This was not the childhood I remembered. I remembered one in which I went to school with straight, tangled hair and hand-me-down clothes. Together with my bratty know-it-all nature, which was reflected even in the scowl on the face of the daintily dressed little girl in the photo, I came to be called *cootie-brain* by jeering classmates. It was a name that stuck with me all the way through the end of fifth grade, which was the year my grandmother died and we were forced to move from her home.

I blamed my mother for both my unhappiness and our family's dysfunctional nature. She was always grouchy and unpleasant. And when my dad came home at night, usually long after I had been put to bed, she was especially angry with him. I would put the pillow over my head to block out the bitter words she screeched, but my mother had a sharp and penetrating voice, and the small cushion was a weak defense.

I was in my mid-30s before the reality that my mother had good reason to be angry hit me, like Thor's hammer coming down on a dim-witted skull. But then children don't see the world through the same eyes as those of an adult, and a child I had still been when I married at barely 16 to escape the discord.

My day of recognition was the one in which I sat, unweeping, at my father's sparsely attended funeral. For the first time, I suddenly knew that my mother had cause to be angry at my always cheerful, but seldom present, father. His early demise at 55, I realized, was probably hastened by his alcoholism, for an alcoholic is what he was, and a gambler as well.

The words of those midnight sessions my mother had with my father, which were especially frightful on Friday nights, replayed themselves in my mind. Sitting at his funeral, I realized my father hadn't come home until he gambled and drank away most, or all, of his weekly paycheck.

He was the reason I wore hand-me-downs and sometimes went to school with holes in my shoes. He was the reason I had been forced to go out in the neighborhood to sell my mother's beautiful crocheting. It was that money, I now realized, that had helped put food on our table. I also remembered the many times when my father, who drove the family car, failed to pick me up as he had promised so I could attend a school event.

I had forgotten all these things, and overlooked them when I was a child, because in person, my dad was always kind and funny and cheerful, everything my mother was not.

I eventually reconciled with my mother, coming to appreciate her many strengths, and realizing that the year I had started first grade, she had given birth to her second child, and then a third one less than a year later. At the same time, she had planted a huge garden every year, canned its bounty, and dutifully taken care of my bedridden grandmother.

While my mother's personality could at times be abrasive, and she was not much of a hugger, her love for us children was real. She expressed it by making sure we had a roof over our heads and a hot-cooked meal on the table every evening.

Even accepting this reality, there was still a lingering, small voice that whispered in my ear, telling me my mother never loved me. Why else would she have allowed me to go to school with my hair looking like it actually had cooties, like my peers had claimed? Yet here was proof, in a tiny black-and-white photo of a girl with ringlets in her hair, that she did love me.

I was surprised to receive the photograph, because the same year I started a new school in sixth grade, I gathered up all the photos of myself and burned them. I had been determined to put my past behind me and start fresh, and the ugly photos of me, with my stringy hair, skinny body, and freckled face, were part of that past. I had no choice but to destroy them.

I realized that the only way this one small picture of me had survived was because it was taken by my aunt, my mother's older sister. Looking at it also brought back another memory long suppressed. It was of me, the first day of school, sitting on a stool with my mother trying to tame my tangled, unruly hair.

The bratty kid I was back then screamed and yelled and cried that she was hurting me. Maybe she was, but I'm sure not as much as I pretended. With the picture of the little girl in ringlets still in my hand, I reheard the words my mother finally uttered that same morning.

"Well from now on, you can comb your hair yourself," she said. Then she put down the comb and walked away, never again to touch my hair.

My going to school with uncombed hair had nothing to do with love. It was all about my mother being a woman who, unlike my dad, stood by her words.

ANGEL'S LANDING

Pat Bean

"I do not understand how anyone can live without
one small place of enchantment to turn to."
— *Marjorie Kinnan Rawlings*

The first time I climbed Angel's Landing in Zion National Park, the five-mile round-trip hike was little more than a walk in the park. I did the climb in about half the time the trail guide said to allow; and I scoffed at the guide's mention that the trail was a "strenuous" one.

My last hike to the top, however, took quite a bit longer than the trail guide indicated. And when I finally reached the summit, where family members and friends had been waiting for some time, I was greeted by a crowd singing "Happy Birthday" to me. It was my 70th birthday, and my kids had put together an impromptu party at the top and invited all the other hikers to join in the fun.

After I managed to catch my breath, and thanked everyone, I looked around. I was, as always, awed and thrilled to the pit of my soul by the magnificent view. Once again I knew I could now handle anything the coming year might throw my way. It was the exact feeling I had experienced more than 30 times. Getting to the top of this Zion Canyon landmark had become, when circumstances allowed, my annual birthday tradition.

The slower pace, which the years have imposed on me, is not something I bemoan. It has given me more time to thoroughly enjoy Mother Nature's bounties, from the trill of a warbler singing in a tree below the trail, to the colorful splash of Indian paintbrush that has pushed its way up through a crack in a rock. Growing older has let me fully appreciate the wisdom of Ursula K. Le Guin's words, "It is good to have an end to journey toward; but it is the journey that matters."

The trail to the top of Angel's Landing begins by crossing a wooden footbridge spanning the Virgin River. The path then meanders gently, rising slowly up from the river's edge while providing a clear view ahead of Angel's Landing. But the rough dirt and rock footpath soon evolves into a series of rapidly rising hairpin turns, which eventually dump hikers out onto a windy lane carved into a rock section of the mountain. Here, one can enjoy a breezy rest while staring down at ant-sized people and what is now just a pale green ribbon of river.

It is at this juncture in the trail, by way of another small bridge, that hikers pass from the mountain on which the trail begins, to the base of Angel's Landing. Depending on the season, the bridge passes over a gushing stream of water or simply a jumble of rocks. I once lost a pair of sunglasses when the water coming down the narrow canyon between the mountains was in high spirits.

On the far side of the bridge, the path gentles and the air cools, making perfect sense of why the canyon between the two mountains was named "Refrigerator." But soon the shady pleasure of the narrow canyon ends, and the trail heads upward again, and up again, through the 21 short, hairpin turns of Walter's Wiggles – yes, I've counted them – and then onto a huge flat-rock area known as Scout's Lookout. Located on the back side of Angel's Landing, this is the stopping point for many hikers, since the last half-mile to the top is a scramble over boulders, and at one point crosses quite a narrow ridge, offering dual bird's eye views of the landscapes below. Thankfully, there's a safety chain to hold on to while making this particular crossing.

It's not unusual, especially when I've stopped to catch my breath and look around, to see a peregrine falcon soaring above – or below me. Peregrine falcons nest each year near the top of the Landing, and seeing one never fails to fill me with wonder.

I've hiked to the top of Angel's Landing in scorching hot weather, in high winds, in rain, once in a snow flurry, and once with a knee wrapped in bandages. I've done the trip alone, and with friends, and once with three young granddaughters in tow.

If I had to pick a favorite climb to the top, it would be the windy one in which I found myself hiking alone. When I reached the top, I had the whole summit to myself, and so it stayed for the entire hour I was up there.

That windy climb was back in the late 1980s. I've not had the pleasure of such solitude since, although I did stand on top one time with only a kindred-soul friend as a companion. That was the snowy climb. She and I had continued on our hike as snowflakes fell around us, and as we neared the summit, the only people we saw were those returning down the trail.

Angel's Landing is a part of me. I have no better words to describe it. All cares and worries vanish when I look out from its summit perch to the Great White Throne opposite, and then down to the tiny string of the Virgin River flowing below. I am home and at peace.

TWO MISTAKES...AND A SURPRISE
Pat Bean

My first and biggest mistake was that I married the wrong man, and then stayed married for 22 years simply because the word *divorce* wasn't in my vocabulary. It was the 1950s, and no one in my family had ever been divorced. When I finally got up the courage to do the deed, basically because I knew my own children would have no respect for me if I didn't, I worried I would repeat my mistake. The worry was intensified because several women among my acquaintances had done exactly that.

This thought preyed on my mind for five years, until I married Michael in the early 1980s. Michael was as opposite from my ex as a hummingbird is to a vulture. But he, too, was the wrong man – and I knew it when I married him. But unlike the first marriage, I have no regrets about this second one. I truly loved Michael. He was the most intelligent man I had ever met, the sexual chemistry between us was fantastic, and Michael always made me feel good about myself, unlike my first husband who made a game of putting me down in public. I felt I would have had more regrets not giving this second marriage a try than I would have had by making yet another mistake.

I originally met Michael in the 1970s, when I was working at Utah State University, with my small salary supporting five young children while at the same time putting my non-working husband through college. It was a big sacrifice for the family, which was never repaid, not even by my ex-husband helping his children with their educational needs. To add insult to injury, during his last year of college my then-husband changed his major from math to journalism, which was my established career. He immediately saw himself as a bigwig editor and me as the cub reporter.

After graduation, my ex got a job at the Logan, Utah, newspaper where I had been working part-time, in addition to my university position. It was here where both of us met Michael. The two of them hated each other instantly, but since both Michael and I were married at the time, I never looked at him twice. Years later, when Michael, also divorced, came to work for the *Standard-Examiner* newspaper in Ogden, Utah, where I was then features editor, we had an instant connection. I know it's not pretty of me, but besides loving him, I think I might have married Michael as revenge on my ex. I know the thought went through my head a time or two, and it always made me smile.

Michael and I dated for the two years we worked at the same paper together in Ogden, then he took a job as news editor at the *Las Vegas Sun*. We married a few months later, and I followed him to Las Vegas, where once again we found ourselves working for the same newspaper. The *Sun* hired me immediately as their features and Sunday editor. It was a fun time for a few months, until Michael's womanizing ways floated to the top of my days. I suspected he had been playing around, but it was finding a Tampax in the toilet – not mine, when I returned home from work one day, that broke my spirit.

I ransacked our apartment and tossed anything important to me into my car, and the rest of the stuff on the floor. And since Michael wasn't home at the time, I left a note that simply said: "Take care of the cat you asshole." I then drove to the newspaper to hand in my immediate resignation, after which I drove out of town and cried all 560 miles back to Ogden, where I crashed on the couch of a good friend.

Michael, through my daughter who was then living in Ogden, got in touch with me a week or so later and asked me to come back. I asked him, through tears that were still falling, if anything would be different. He honestly replied, "No." A couple of weeks later, he hired a truck and drove the rest of my belongings and furniture to me at my new apartment in Ogden.

From the first mistake of marrying the wrong man, I learned not to repeat mistakes. From the second mistake of marrying the wrong man, I learned that I could always change my mind, that a decision didn't have to be permanent, and that I was strong enough to handle the world alone.

For many years after that, I clung to the hope that I would find a true soul mate. Then one day, I woke up and realized what a great life I had, and that I had been sabotaging any relationships that held promise. Perhaps it was because, subconsciously at least, I knew I was happiest when single. I gave too much of myself away when I was attached to a man.

Now, as I write about my marriage mistakes for the first time, I'm suddenly realizing my true soul mate is myself. Perhaps I should have written about these chapters in my life earlier. But then I do love to read stories with surprise endings. I also love being a writer. How else would I have discovered the real me?

I AM 80

Pat Bean

I would be naïve and foolish if I did not acknowledge, after eight decades of life, that there are fewer years ahead of me than behind me.

It's not something I dwell on but accept, although such acceptance is still tinged with a hunger to make every day of the rest of my life meaningful.

Meaningful to an 80-year-old, however, is not the same as meaningful to a 10-year-old wanting to be loved; a 20-year-old full of fanciful ideas of being the perfect wife and mother; a 30-year-old focused on a career; a 40-year-old freed of responsibility who wants to have fun and an adventure or two; a 50-year-old who is still looking for a soul mate; a 60-year-old looking forward to retirement and travel; or even a 70-year-old who fulfills a lifetime dream of traveling across America's backroads and writes a book about it. Those years were the seasons of an active life, full of rainbows and potholes that created the 80-year-old sitting here and struggling to write something meaningful today.

The early years came with a lot of tears, hard work, and finally acceptance that life is not fair, a difficult understanding for an optimist who prefers looking at the world through rose-colored glasses. At 80, the glasses are off. I still see kindness and love in this world, but I can no longer deny that it exists, side-by-side, with hate and evil.

I find it unbelievable that I still have hope for a world full of peace and harmony, even while the drum beat of reality forces acknowledgement that it won't happen in my lifetime, nor even in the lifetimes of my great-grandchildren. But just perhaps the world will awaken and their children's-children's-children will have it.

Meaningful to this 80-year-old would be to do something to make that future actually happen, yet all I can come up with is to be kind, and urge others to do the same. It's a tiny grain of sand in an unending universe, and so I look for other ways to spend my eighth decade.

I spent 37 years as a journalist, writing about the goings-on in the world, beginning at the peak of the Vietnam War and ending with our country going into Iraq a second time. These years provide the background for a memoir I've started called *Between Wars*. Writing it feels meaningful.

As does reading the three large bins of clippings and journals I've saved over the past half century. Finally, at 80 years old, I am rereading them. They are helping me connect the dots of my journey through life, a byway that saw a high school dropout become an award-winning journalist, and then an 80-year-old who is blessed to be loved, even if she never found that soul mate.

Socrates believed that an unexamined life is not worth living. I'm not sure I totally agree, but I'm having my eyes opened as I examine my life of the past 80 years. Looking at it through the lens of time, I've gained a new appreciation for myself but also realize I had many faults and made many mistakes, and was never the hero I occasionally thought I was.

I like having this season of contemplation. It makes being 80 years old worth the journey. If the years are kind to me, I'm sure I will continue to make more mistakes, but I also hope that I continue to learn and grow every day along the way. Being 80 is not bad at all.

MUST HAVE BEEN THE STARS

Ariela Zucker

We met in the desert. Primal land, the way it was created when the world began, no frills or decorations, no human hand to soften the creation by adding parks or sitting areas with shade. This was an ancient land where the mountains still reached the sky and touched the stars, a million sparkling mirrors, not paled by artificial lights.

And one man, and one woman.

Later, I was not sure if it was the stars, the water softly licking my fingers, or the mountains fiercely jutting out. It could have been his Jeep. The memory moves a warm, tingly sensation that spreads inside me. It has been a while since I felt like that.

The dusty monster roared and thrust like a horse ready to dislodge. I felt the contained power going to erupt while sitting in the front seat next to him, one leg thrown nonchalantly over the edge as if I do not take it seriously, as I would treat a ride in the city, not the big deal that it was.

He controlled the beast with ease. One hand on the wheel and the other, on the back of my seat, while not quite touching felt heavy with radiating heat. We rode up to the mountains, all the way to the edge where only a few breaths of air separated us from a deadly dive, and we flirted with the echoes coming back at us from the sheer walls of canyons, fluttering like the puffy white clouds over the salty azure water. I was consumed by excitement.

Was it love at first sight?

Twenty-four hours earlier he had been a stranger, unknown as the mountains and the water and the stars. He claimed his right with unchallenged assurance. Like a tired traveler that stakes a stretch of land never seen before calling it home. I gave him one look and succumbed. No words of introduction exchanged; no explanations needed. This was a sealed deal before it was signed up.

The romance lasted for three breathtaking days,

Then it was drawn-out for three months,

And then it was dead.

I kept blaming the stars. No one can see the stars in the city. In the dim light, without their enchanting sparkle, he was robbed of his glamour, his confidence, his roaring Jeep, his power over me.

His hair, light like the sun at noon,

His eyes, dark blue like the ocean,

And at night, his hands in mine sending waves of warmth and transmitting safety. His hands everywhere like the warm sand under us, like the soft wind caressing my flushed face.

Was it the stars? Or perhaps the clear warm water where the reflection of the stars fused with the tiny silvery fish that streamed through my fingers. But it could have also been the mountains; black silhouettes that penetrated a dark velvety night.

When the past is brighter than the present it is a sure sign that you went over the tipping point, and you are officially old. I know that to be true, but I am not distressed. The passing time granted me images, so clear and detailed I can pull them out with ease and flip through them like a favorite picture album. After all the years, three hypnotizing days are still etched in my mind. I pull them out, the memories, the views; one by one I suck at them, sweet candies. I draw any sweetness left.

SPRING AGAIN

Shelley Johnson Carey

The magic moments of young love—
Dizzying dances, sparkling kisses
Awakening with music floating from your tongue.

A tender sprout pushes through melting frost
Grows toward the moment's warmth
And blossoms into
The We,
The Us,
A Pair.

Two sparrows using bits of jeweled dreams
To build shelter from the squalls of yet to be.

Later, slipping through crevices of neglect and time
Come invasions of those
Who gnaw at love's foundation
To harvest the bounty for themselves.

So, is the secret of happiness
To keep a half note tucked inside your heart
That can break free
And find its way back to your mouth?
Will its sweet sound make spring come again?

PANGS

Marilea C. Rabasa

When we were still teachers in Virginia more than a decade ago, it was a rare summer that my partner, Gene, and I didn't visit one of our wondrous national parks in the United States. In another life, I'd seen much of the world in the Foreign Service, yet had known little of my own country.

But Gene had, and he was determined to share with me the wealth of his experiences. He has loved and appreciated the diversity of many of them, from the Adirondacks to Capitol Reef to Yosemite. And the sheer beauty of them is enough to take your breath away.

One hot July in 2007, we traveled almost as far away from Virginia as you can get on the North American continent. We flew to Vancouver, British Columbia, to see the northern Rockies. On the highway to Whistler, where the Winter Olympics were held one year, Gene shouted suddenly, "Stop the car! I want to show you a beautiful lake. Drop dead gorgeous, jes' like you," planting a wet kiss on my cheek.

Well, he was a charmer. That's one reason I fell for him. But I was the sensible one. Mix dreamer with practical and sometimes you just get vinegar....

Gene felt we needed to get far away that summer. A difficult personal challenge was proving to be too much for me to handle. I thought if I could knead the pain out of me by climbing a mountain, I might start to feel better. But I wasn't twenty-five anymore. The physical challenge facing me now would be considerable. And the spiritual one, even greater.

Fifteen switchbacks: I counted 'em. It was a long hike. The trail seemed to go for a mile before it mercifully turned the other way. Is that fifteen miles? Or does it just seem like that? We were backpacking on an elevated trail. And we had full loads. There's only one way to go, and that's up.

After a while I started fantasizing about being airlifted to our destination: powerful fairies swooping down and grabbing us by the shoulders, bypassing the trail and slicing straight up through the thickly stacked trees, gently placing our grateful bodies down at the campsite and returning to the air without so much as a thank you or a tip. Then I tripped over a rock and awoke from my reverie.

"Gene, for Chrissake, we didn't plan this at all! We should have gone shopping first and gotten enough food to sustain us. How are we gonna live on so little protein?" I yelled, already anticipating disaster. My gnawing hunger brought out the worst in me, and my recovery was going to be sorely tested.

"Darlin', when you see the turquoise lake at the top, you won't care," he assured me.

"Yes I will," I whined, "Oh, yes I will...."

Every day when we wake up, life happens to us. We can't escape from what comes. How we face it, the choices we make, with or without a problem to wrestle with, is a test of our mettle. I'm like everyone else: I have strengths and weaknesses. On this particular hike, out of the many we have taken, I failed to meet our difficulties with any grace. But, as with most of the failures littering my deck overlooking the water, this one in the Canadian Rockies contained a gem of wisdom to add to the many others I've collected over the years. It's a highly recurrent one.

About halfway up, tired, sweaty, and irritable, we decided to lighten our loads by eating our hamburgers. That was a grave error in judgment, cutting down on our food supply so early in the trip. We would dream of eating those hamburgers two days later when we were running out of food and the stamina to keep hiking.

Another mistake was impulsively starting the hike at two o'clock in the afternoon. The only thing that might have saved us in that regard was the lingering light at that latitude in the summer months. But we would be cursed again, this time by the weather; we would not experience any evening lightness.

Gene and I soldiered on. We were both too proud to turn around and go back down. I kept thinking of that turquoise lake, and Gene kept belting out arias from Samuel Ramey in "Mefistofele." Not a good choice, but I guess we were wrestling with the devil in some ways.

My own dark side was coming out in glossy Technicolor.

Five hours later, the sky grew dark and we knew what was coming. We got caught in a drenching downpour. If I'd adopted a better attitude,

I'd have been grateful for the free air conditioning about to cool us off. We were near the end of the trail and came upon the lake Gene had been talking about. He marveled at it through the trees and pointed it out to me. But I didn't care. My stomach was already growling. And I was soaked. I was in no mood for silver linings.

As we arrived at the campsite and prepared to pitch our tent, we were presented with one: the rain had let up just in time to appreciate our elevated spot overlooking Lake Garibaldi and Sphinx Glacier. A gorgeous spot that Gene photographed multiple times. It's still one of his favorite photographs. But I was not yet able to distinguish between happiness and joy.

So began three days of wilderness camping and hiking on a subsistence level diet. It was necessary to ration all our food. Ration our food? On a demanding hike in the Canadian Rockies? That's the one thing we should have had enough of. Primitive camping carries with it enough discomforts without adding that to the list. Gene has always added to his own backpack the weight of extra food so we'd never run short.

This was not the first nor would it be the last time we were swept away and allowed good judgment to take a back seat.

The next day we walked around that lake, eating half a sandwich each for lunch. I learned to eat slowly, savoring every morsel, which is how I should eat anyway. I never appreciated gorp so much. Dinner was half rations again and sleep was fitful. I was hungry.

We tackled the real focus of our trip on our second day at the campsite: a demanding trek up to the base of the Black Tusk, a volcanic neck on the shoulder of Mt. Garibaldi. We made it, trudged all the way up to the snow line. Took congratulatory pictures. Then we went back down with little to look forward to but half a sandwich.

The thing about hunger is, like pain, it's a nasty distraction. Loading up on plenty of filling food every day, like most intelligent hikers, I should have been enjoying the breathtaking views. Instead, I was guzzling water to quell my hunger pangs—and dreaming about food.

The third morning, humbled for a couple of seasoned backpackers, we asked people for any extra food as they were packing out. They gave us apples and more gorp. And sorry looks.

Flying down those same fifteen switchbacks the next day, we jumped into the car and barreled down the road to a Chinese restaurant in Squamish. Spring rolls the width of thermoses, chicken and this, noodles and that, we gobbled up each dish like it was our last meal. Food had never tasted so good.

I'm certain I've never experienced true hunger or anything close to starvation. But food for the soul, that was what I was missing those three days. Had I been more willing to recognize silver linings in the midst of difficulties, I'd have ignored the discomfort and focused on the stunning landscape surrounding me. That would have been a deliberate and preferable choice.

Happiness involves many good feelings and happenings: nice weather, friendly people, a delicious meal. But I have found in my experience that it's necessary to dig down much deeper to access the channels to joy.

On this Canadian hike the gem of wisdom most shimmering to me was that despite the outward and transitory nature of many things, both pleasant and otherwise, the joy that comes from gratitude at having persevered through any difficulty is most profound—and the most salient lesson of all.

THE CASTING
Katelynn Butler

2016
I found you, in my travels, in that dark corner, writing poetry.
Now, I swim in these channels you've built for us,
Knowing I belong in the heart of the flow, and you in the shaping of it.

We argue like smoke, swirls of words and abstractions,
So thick, accurately representative of the source of heat… I am here
    now. Then
I feel the Universe crack wide open. Everything beautiful is painful.
I already know his heartbeat. I have no name for him yet, except
    "powerful one."

I suffocate myself to stay – crippling, breaking love. Holes in the walls
    love.
I wore the red dress, the favorite you don't care to remember.
With the boots that weren't made for walking on egg shells
Or through the mercury of your eyes.

2017
He has been here a month now. They took him from me, away.
When they returned him three hours later, I was unsure he was mine,
Like a wild animal, whose young are taken from her nest before
    bonding…

You threaten the fate of wrists and ropes
While you water the bed sheets with the spit of your hate
Screaming at me, cowering and holding our child.

I am grateful for the way the wind sticks my hair to my cheeks
When I cry on a warm night under the stars.
I am grateful for the body's ability to expel toxins
and hold the power of memory for courageous action.

2018

I've done it. I found myself in the burnt ashes of you – Which of us
    lit the match?
Every day I feel incompetent – because I am.
Children should have two parents.
And loving safety
From rejection. And guns. And the 15th beer.

I am shells discarded along the path. Perhaps if I collect them all
I will see the mass of substance I yearn for within their hollows.
You still bind my chest with ropes I can't touch.

2019

To my true love: I can't stop feeling your giggle
Rolling out of your throat into my heart for the rest of our lives.
I cry rocking you to sleep, "Dance me to your beauty with a burning
    violin…"
I watch you throw clean clothes at the line, shouting "got it!" as they
    fall onto rocks.
I wrap my fingers in your ringlets as you hop into the bench next to me
To point out the bird I could barely see.
I dance you around in my arms; only you know what it's like to see
    me dance with abandon.
I admire you as you vocalize "Mae Among the Stars"
I thought the yellow truck in your hands was keeping you
    from hearing the book.
I can't wait for you to awaken me at 5:30 a.m. to crawl into bed with
    me
And restlessly force me to lie there and love you, since I won't be
    sleeping.
I am forever with child.
And you are forever with me.
And that is enough.

WESTERNS
Claire McCabe

They watch cowboy shows;
he likes the rifles, dirty boots
and spurs. She cries when
the horses' mouths twist
at the bit's jerk.

She's felt supple lips
lift a sugar cube from her palm;
she's pressed her face against the horses'
harsh hairs softened with scent
of hay and sweat.

He thrills as the roped calves thud to the ground
in a powder of dust, their hooves bound by hands
hard as tanned leather. She hears the bleating
cries as the scorch of the branding
sears their hides.

From the first, he wants
the rough and tumble, the flanking,
the tie down. She wants the horses
and the calves
to be free.

One day, she'll don
dun-colored pants,
a denim shirt,
and summon the earth
and sky.

She'll gallop the desert, hard
til hooves split
on rocks, and mane
tears away;
she'll race and race far
as the closing sun,
and spin in the grit
of beginning
and sand.

MAKE IT HAPPEN

Marilyn H. Collins

*Stuck in the wrong job with the wrong man
—she decided to take a chance*

Alexus felt lost in all that empty space. Void of house or tree, the dusty miles spread in every direction from her parked car. Not a human-made sound gave warmth to the cold world around her. A breeze rattled the dry scrub brush. Shrilly calling to each other, two hawks circled overhead.

She had wanted to get away from the stand-still traffic of Washington, DC—horns blaring, radios pounding out loud music, and people yelling for a cab. And Jake.

Out of cell phone range, she spread her map across the hood of her car and tried to figure out how close she'd come to the small town outside of Albuquerque—her destination. She'd seen paintings of the Sandia Mountains that rose from the stark desert floor. Brilliant yellows and reds of cactus flowers added contrast to the scene. Would she be able to capture on canvas that blinding light and give credit to the vast space? Or had she lost her touch in her confined job as a graphic artist working strictly to meet the client's changing needs? She determined to find out.

Her savings wouldn't last long. She'd better make something happen soon. First, a cheap place with good light where she could set up her studio and paint every free minute. Second, a job. She'd stay too busy to think of Jake—her office mate and significant other, who moaned for time to write and play his music. Time seemed not so much his problem as lack of faith in himself.

"You're living a dream, Alexus," Jake had warned her as they munched a quick lunch in the staff break room. "Fantasies don't come true."

"How do you know if you've never tried? I'm twenty-six years old and have never once taken a risk. I feel my creative juices draining away. There's nothing left at the end of my day."

She covered his hand with hers, "Why don't you come with me? Bring your guitar and computer. Stuff your dreams in a backpack and let's take a chance together."

But he hadn't come.

Ok, get a grip and bring your dreams down to earth, Alexus told herself. She got back in the car and turned south off I-40. Twenty minutes later, she stopped her car on a low knoll. She could see the small town below. Didn't look like much. Just four or five rows of buildings lined each side of a wide center street. There seemed no need for more than one stoplight. Surely there was a place to stay, but finding a job might be more difficult.

She drove into town, pulling up by a sort of bed and breakfast— certainly not your glass-of-wine-at-sunset and gourmet-meal style place. But the sign out front seemed friendly—"Roadrunner Inn."

As she got out of the car, a voice said, "You look ready to stop for the day." Turning her head, she easily found the source. A tall, deeply tanned man was putting a coat of blue paint on the porch columns.

Putting his brush down, he smiled, "I'm Robert Libeman." The paint color matched the blue of his eyes. "Come in and I'll show you around."

"Thanks. I'm Alexus Roth."

She followed him up the steps, "Why 'Roadrunner?'"

"I lived the roadrunner life once, taking to the road as fast as I could to get away. This is where I stopped and decided to open a place for folks like me. They may not stay long but, instead of splattering off the canyon floors of their lives, this'll be a safe haven to catch their breath."

He opened the door for her. "Watch the paint."

Inside, the inn welcomed her with deep leather chairs and a long couch covered with a bright plaid quilt. Paintings of desert scenes and muted sunsets filled the walls. The large windows revealed the porch curving around the house.

"There are four rooms upstairs," Robert said. "The couple who own the coffee shop rent one room full time, and the other room is taken for the weekend. Then I have the downstairs room in the front. Each has their own private bath."

"I really want a room with a lot of light and space where I can paint," Alexus said.

"I converted a large room in the back to a bedroom with its own private porch. Would you like to see it?"

He led the way, picking up a brochure detailing the inn as they walked. "I offer reasonable rates by the night, week, or a special long-term rate for those who want to stay a while."

Stepping into the sunny, spacious room, Alexus caught her breath. Sheer curtains hung by the windows. Distant mountains rose straight up from the desert floor. A bright yellow coverlet on the bed matched the two chairs and picked up the tiny, yellow cactus flowers in the wallpaper. An outside door opened into a cozy porch with its own sky-blue swing. Lots of room to set up her easel.

He turned toward her with a grin, "This desert is full of people who've come to live out their dreams. And others who've just kept running. So, which will it be?"

Alexus saw the challenge in his eyes. "I'll take it. For how long depends on finding a job in town. Do you know anyone who's hiring?"

"We may seem off the beaten track," said Robert. "But the town is full during tourist season. Then we have two big restaurants open. One south-of-the-border style food—lives up to its fiery name, 'Unquenchable.' The other 'Sam and Jill's,' is a true western steak house that draws crowds to its whole-beef outdoor barbeques.

Three galleries are busy during the season, and sidewalk artists are popular. 'The Necessary' serves as a grocery, hardware, and clothing store year round. But the other two bed-and-breakfasts are closed during the winter."

"Waiting for summer to come may be too long for me," said Alexus. "I'll need a job before then."

As they walked back toward the front of the house, Robert continued, "Almena owns two of the galleries not open to the public this time of year. However, she stays busy through the shoulder season with catalog sales, mailing art and prints all over the world. She might need some help. I'd be happy to give her a call."

Alexus smiled her thanks. Impossible dreams one day, a world filled with possibilities the next, she thought. And one good-looking road-runner who understands risking it all.

Whatever lay ahead, she knew for certain she didn't want what she'd left behind.

STARTING OVER
Charlotte Wlodkowski

There was no hurry. She sat sipping morning coffee and munching a breakfast bagel. This was the first McDonald's she'd visited that played her kind of music. She found it invigorating. Although she wondered how the older customers felt about rock and roll. She surmised they preferred crooners. The music reminded her that she had a lot of energy to spread around. The woman would have danced in the aisle with Rod Stewart, but she didn't think the other patrons would understand her joy. Within a few weeks, she would be free of a marriage that held her for years, choked her with silence and stifled her spirit. For now, she was content to sit and let her body sway with the lyrics.

Most conversations bouncing around the restaurant were deep voices telling old jokes. The few older women sat and whispered. She wondered why the difference, then remembered the older generation of women were raised to be in the background. A few facial wrinkles appeared as she silently thanked her female relatives for teaching her independence.

Lately, her laptop screen scrolled house after house with details of each to prompt the buyer to visit. Hours went by before she required a break. Looking for an affordable house to make a home was all-consuming. There was no returning to the split-level, where she'd spent thirty-plus years. Her new-to-her home required a garage and dining room. Owing money any longer than a month was unthinkable, but she was mentally prepared for the challenge. Most of the time, she was comfortable with her soon-to-be-divorced status. At times though, doubt robbed her confidence and she took a few steps backwards.

Her life was a series of emotional struggles, except for a ten-year period between her forties and fifties. As a member of an organization, her focus fell upon its activities. Being elected chapter president validated her worth. This gave her permission to introduce new ideas, rejuvenate and empower its members.

She was now counted as an older citizen. One would think her life to be mundane. She would admit to only a short time of easy and predictable living. It was inevitable that adversity lurked and jumped into her lap. It was as though mischief and discourse waited until she was content and then struck. There was no sitting on a sofa or watching television.

The next step will be a big one. She will need to negotiate a house full of furniture. She had ignored offers to take the dark, heavy, and memory-filled pieces from her former residence. Instead, she will choose light-colored, contemporary furnishings. She'll add as much red as delights her, and accents of yellow if it pleases her.

This woman promises she will share the benefits of living alone with other disillusioned, divorced women. The next ten years belong to her.

FINDING BUSTER
Jude Walsh

My divorce was a miserable experience. I never, ever thought divorce was even a remote possibility in my life. Even after years of legal wrangling and much bitterness, I did not truly believe it would happen. I thought at some point my husband would wake up, come to his senses, and appreciate the life and family we created together, the love we shared. That did not occur. By the time of the final court hearing I was feeling depleted, rejected, and vulnerable. From the moment I discovered that he was having an affair, that later became having a mistress, he went from being my best friend, staunchest ally, and life mate, to a cruel stranger. He made it clear there was nothing he valued from our life together, dismissing my attempts to remind him of what we had. At every turn he, as a lawyer himself, negotiated down to the last dollar. My support was calculated to the one hundredth of a point. There was no acknowledgement of my contribution to our financial wealth. At that point I felt rejected and devalued. What felt worse was that it no longer felt good to recall what were precious memories from our marriage. I was filled with doubt. Was anything real about the marriage? Had I been living an illusion all those years? I could no longer trust my own judgment or perception of reality. The only way to survive that, to allow myself time to heal and rebuild, to find myself again was to block out those memories. Thinking about them triggered distress and hurt and did me no good. So I made the choice to live in the present and move forward one day at a time.

Divorce is similar to death in that grief is involved. I was mourning the end of the marriage and the loss of what I thought was my future. I was grieving my loss of trust and the joy of all the memories I once treasured and now doubted.

As time passes, the intensity of that kind of discomfort eases. But the loss remains and the emptiness of the past isolates.

Ten years post divorce –

I had just hiked for an hour at my local Metropark and was driving to McDonald's, looking forward to a refreshing iced tea. Then out of the corner of my eye, I saw it.

A tan Volkswagen Beetle in pristine condition. The bug was pulling out of a parking place in front of the local barbershop. I hung a quick right and tried to follow the car to at least get a picture. You see I learned to drive, at age 21, in a tan Volkswagen beetle. My then fiancé and I bought it together, even though I did not drive, and named him Buster. As our wedding date grew closer, it became evident that I needed to get to some appointments on my own so he taught me to drive and I took the test and got my driver's license. Seeing that car opened a chink in my armor. That small memory triggered another. I remembered my first lesson in a nearly empty parking lot where I was learning how to back up. My fiancé quietly said "Stop" as I eased backward, then a bit more forcefully, "Stop!" I punched the brake, startled and irritated. We got out of the car and I realized I was inches away from whacking the only other car in the lot! I thought about how we laughed together and how relaxed and happy we were with one another. Whoa! Stopped that thought. Like I said, I stay firmly in the present. I had learned to look forward with future plans but still stayed firmly out of the past.

A week later, I was driving past that same barbershop and there the car was again, this time in a parking space. I drive this route frequently and had never seen the car before and now saw it twice in seven days. I pulled over, parked and took out my phone to snap a picture. Just as I snapped it, a man came out of the barbershop and asked me what I was doing. It was his car, of course. I explained that I once had one just like it. He said he never drives it anywhere without at least one person approaching him. He then told me a charming story.

A woman approached him like I did and shared that when her now middle-aged son was an infant and would not go to sleep, she would put him in the tiny baggage well behind the rear seat of her VW and drive him just a few blocks and he would fall asleep. He asked her if she would like to take the car for a brief drive. I thought to myself, this is a pretty trusting guy. He handed the keys to his collectable car to a woman he just met. She drove the car around the block and returned the keys to him, tears streaming down her face. He said he shed a few tears of his own. I knew what he meant as I was blinking back tears myself.

He then asked me if I would like to get behind the wheel. I said no, telling myself it was because I was too hot and sweaty from hiking to get into his immaculate car. He did snap a picture of me standing next to what I now perceived as Buster. I thanked him and headed to McDonald's.

Once there I pulled out my phone to take a look at the picture. And something in me broke. Memory after memory after memory of my early married life played in my head. Driving to the New Jersey shore for our honeymoon. Our first camping trip to Nova Scotia where we called from a phone booth with a two-digit number to find out if our best friend's first child had arrived. She had! A near miss on the Massachusetts turnpike when an eighteen-wheel truck blew a tire. Driving ten hours from home to a new city where my husband would start law school. So many memories. Then I felt it. A bit of joy, a bit of nostalgia, and I smiled.

It seems like I had things backward. I didn't find Buster. Buster found me.

ONE WOMAN'S LIFE
Marilyn H. Collins

Screen door slamming, my three raggedy little girls burst into the kitchen with skirt hems dragging, a button on a shirt missing, and nails with dirt peeking out from the day. Fortunately, they didn't start out the day that way. Tiny purple and yellow flowers clutched in their fists were gifts to me. They loved the outdoors and climbed trees, waded in the creek, and played in the woods or surrounding fields.

How did this become my world? I grew up reading Latin, writing poetry, studying ancient Greek history, and accomplishing higher math.

My mother held the honor of Magna cum Laude from the Academy in town.

But life often does not follow the path where you first begin. My engagement to Frank didn't last long. My fault. He just wasn't for me. Time passed and I took notice of the tall, skinny man who lived a quarter mile down the road. His humor and blue eyes caught my attention. He worked hard but had little money. He finally asked me to the movies.

"What's playing?" I asked, not realizing how inappropriate that really sounded. I would hear that phrase jokingly repeated into the future.

I grew up with fine clothes, handcrafted furniture, and lived on a hundred-acre farm next to the 20 acres my husband-to-be would one day own. The excitement of getting married and going to California on our honeymoon distracted me from thinking of how different life would become. Elmer was romantic and picked Valentine's Day for our wedding. He wore a blue wool suit. I wore an embroidered green satin dress with an attached fox fur-collar.

We spent our first night snug in the old farmhouse listening to the logs crackling inside the red-hot, potbellied stove. Just at dawn, the clanging of pots and pans and explosions of fireworks woke us. The shivaree had begun, with neighbors from surrounding farms gathering to celebrate our wedding.

February was not a bad month for traveling to California. But the dust and heat swirling inside our Model T Ford coming back to Arkansas that summer wore on me and my unborn baby. I lost our first child. We had no money for a proper headstone. So we used a lovely, black onyx stone placed beneath an oak tree to mark her simple grave on the point of land overlooking our creek. Her name was "Rose." I could never again bear to speak her name, but carried her in my heart—always.

Two more girls came along and I thought, thank goodness, I was finished with all that. But, no, here came another girl born in the humid heat of an August night. Wet sheets hung across the windows to help cool the room as the breeze filtered in from the sweltering dark. The doctor didn't arrive on time, so the nurse became my midwife.

Fortunately, my mother took care of the girls so I could go back to work. I had my degree in business and worked in town for the First National Bank. I greeted people in a business dress and wearing red, high-heeled shoes. On Sundays, I helped out at the First Baptist Church as the Adult Sunday School Department Secretary.

My life at home was different. We had a big garden with the best red tomatoes and lots of other vegetables. Our Rock Island hens, a couple of cows, and an Australian Collie who answered to "Ike" made up the rest of our homestead.

Elmer worked as an electrician and often traveled out of town to a job. I canned food, gathered eggs with the girls, and milked cows. Clothes washed and hand-wrung smelled so fresh and clean on the line. I ironed everything—even the sheets and Elmer's T-shirts and shorts—while listening to soap operas like "Just Plain Bill" or "Stella Dallas" on the radio. Don't get me wrong—I've never been very domestic—just did what needed doing. Finally, I became a good cook. My husband like to tease me with a round, green rock—from our early married days—which he kept on a shelf in the kitchen. He proudly labeled it, "Ruby's first biscuit."

Black walnut trees grew in the yard. The girls cracked and shelled the nuts, which were perfect for stirring into chocolate fudge. Each time they argued over who would get to lick the spoon and pan. Waiting for the hot fudge to cool on the back porch before cutting took the most patience.

On hot summer nights with all the windows open, I'd sit at the old, upright grand piano and play hymns and we'd all sing. Neighbors far down the road gathered on their porches and listened—maybe they sang along, too. But on long, winter evenings, we'd sit around the kitchen table and play dominoes, Old Maid and Authors cards, or checkers. At Christmas, we'd spread out and work a thousand-piece puzzle on a long, yellow wood table—the same "watermelon table" we put out under the elm tree in summer.

Another side of me played out in my imagination and memory of my life before all this. I had my big wooden trunk in the barn attic filled with books—higher math, Latin, French, and the classics. Rare china from Germany, Prussia, and England filled the rest of the space. The girls loved to go through and read the books or play with the dishes. Our Sunday dinner table was always set with my mother's best china. Stuck in the corner of the trunk were postcards from my travel with friends to the beach, mountains, or big cities. Pictures showed us taking long walks down railroad tracks or enjoying a picnic at the lake near my home. There seemed little outlet now to explore my interests with friends, as my time stayed filled with the day-to-day.

Our girls turned out to be talented, college graduates, and later held professional positions in other states.

Life gradually changed again. Time finally opened for Elmer and me to better know and enjoy each other. I realized that he was probably the smartest one of us all. Not the "college educated" one—but very creative, resourceful, and fun. He taught the men's Bible class for years and was quite a Bible scholar. He served in WWI, traveled around this country and in Europe—and worked as a cowboy, prospector, and bit-movie actor on the west coast before settling down in Arkansas and marrying me. Finally, I could travel with him as he worked up and down the East Coast. We'd often stop at historic sites or explore fun places along the way.

Elmer's mother always told him, "Never sell the land," a common wisdom of the day—especially in the South. When he retired, we returned to the farm. We both had good health. I became involved in local historical groups, and made friends who shared my love of history and research. Elmer enjoyed working on his inventions or repairing one car or another.

In the evening, we walked around the lower pasture on a path Elmer cleared. We'd always pause to watch the moon come up over the "Moon Trees" as we called them. Ending the day with a little romance.

Did I have a good life? Not the one I'd imagined. But I had a husband who told me, "I love you," every time he left the house, children who turned out well, and we ended the day in beauty. What do you think?

AMELIA, THE WASP, AND ME

Sarah Byrn Rickman

At 13, I discovered Amelia Earhart. I fell in love with airplanes and the whole idea of women in flight. That day, I began a journey that, 50 years later, led to publication of my first book – *The Originals: The Women's Auxiliary Ferrying Squadron of WWII.*

Our ninth grade English textbook contained biographies of famous Americans. Amelia was the lone woman included. "The Girl in Brown Who Walks Alone" told the story of the painfully private yet conspicuously public woman who helped set my feet, and those of so many young women, on the path to flight. Like fellow aviator Charles Lindbergh, in the '30s she had captured the imagination of Depression-weary, hero-worshipping America.

That Halloween, I dressed as Amelia – my riding jodhpurs and boots (both appropriately brown), a 1930s-vintage, leather flying helmet and goggles, a newly purchased cloth imitation of a leather flight jacket that I wheedled out of my mother, and a white nylon scarf – not the long, flowing, silk number worn with such panache by early aviators.

A Mysterious Disappearance

I read everything I could find on the ill-fated Amelia and her mysterious disappearance on July 2, 1937, off Howland Island in the Pacific Ocean. Rumors suggested her around-the-world flight was cover for a spy mission; that she was checking on Japanese defenses for President Roosevelt.

Had she been shot down? Was she taken prisoner by the Japanese? Was there a clandestine romance between Amelia and her navigator Fred Noonan? What we know is she, Noonan, and her twin-engine Lockheed Electra disappeared without a trace.

After World War II, the search for her began anew. The hunt continues to this day.

To a 13-year-old, Amelia's life was the stuff of which adventure and romance was made. And *flying!* Forty years after encountering Amelia between the pages of a book, within the space of a few hours, I moved, irrevocably, into the world of women in aviation.

"Did you leave the local newspaper?" Joan Hrubec – administrator for the International Women's Air and Space Museum – asked.

"Yes." A wannabe novelist, I had – after considerable soul searching – resigned my editor's job.

A Chance to Fly!

Joan offered me work writing and promoting the museum, housed in the Dayton, Ohio, suburban community where I lived. IWASM collects stories and memorabilia of women flyers – from Amelia on down to the present. They are preserving those stories for future generations to learn about these incredible women who thought and acted outside the box in the 1920s '30s, '40s, on up to our present generation of female pilots.

Saying "yes" changed my life.

The museum offered three lectures a year featuring accomplished women pilots. When I attended my first one, I immediately saw an opportunity they were missing. "You need to be videotaping your lecture series for posterity," I told Joan. "You need to film these pioneering women while you have them here."

I went to the program director at the local public access cable TV station. Dave Gordon, Joan and I formed a team. We planned three lectures a year, to be taped in the Miami Valley Cable Council's studio and shown to the community on public access channels.

Twelve Programs for Posterity

Joan, Dave and I produced twelve shows in all – four years' worth. The first featured the museum's indomitable president, Nancy Hopkins Tier, then 81 and still flying. In November 1929, 20-year-old Nancy Hopkins joined Amelia and 97 other women pilots to form the women's f lying organization the Ninety-Nines – so named for their charter membership and, with roughly 5,000 members, still thriving today.

We featured individuals like U.S woman aerobatic champion Patty Wagstaff and the first woman jet airliner pilot, Emily Warner. We hosted panels: the WASP – the women pilots of WWII; women corporate pilots; a panel from the International Society of Women Airline Pilots (ISA+21). A Medevac helicopter pilot and her flight nurse talked about their roles rescuing the wounded in Desert Storm. A woman tanker pilot related her Desert Storm experiences flying a tanker engaged in refueling fighter aircraft in the air. These women were among the earliest women pilots to see combat.

I overcame my aversion to the probing eye of the TV camera and moderated several panels – incredible learning experiences.

And then I Met Nancy

Through the WASP panel in January 1992, I met the woman who became my mentor, Nancy Batson Crews – one of the first 28 women hired to ferry aircraft for the Army in World War II. Nancy and I hit it off. Later, when I asked if I might write her biography, her answer was: "Sarah, I want you to write about the Women's Auxiliary Ferrying Squadron (WAFS) and Nancy Love." The WAFS later became known as WASP (Women Airforce Service Pilots), and Nancy Love was the WAFS founder and leader.

No resource existed that explained the historical difference between the WAFS and the WASP. Nor was there a biography of Nancy Love. Both were mine for the writing. "Do it," Joan urged.

Nancy Crews and I formed a partnership and I began writing. My first book, *The Originals,* was born the night I picked her up at the Dayton airport. *The Originals* – the WAFS' and Nancy's story – was published July 2001 and the second edition came out in 2017.

It all began with Amelia!

A TALE OF TWO COMMITTEES
Susan D. Corbin

I started graduate school in Communication Studies at 40, as one answer to my midlife crisis. Seven years later, I was facing the last challenge of my graduate program, the doctoral dissertation defense. I was dreading sitting before a committee of five august professors and defending my research. I don't think well under pressure and this was going to be the most pressure-filled day of my life. At this meeting, they would tell me whether my research was good enough to earn a Ph.D. What I had not expected was dealing with the second committee, the one in my head.

The meeting was set for Friday, August 28, 1998 at 10 a.m. in the Dean's Conference Room. Usually these meetings were held in the conference room within the departmental office. However, due to scheduling issues, I had to reserve the Dean's Conference Room. There were no friendly faces around and it was the DEAN's conference room, filled with big chairs around a large glass-topped table and portraits of dour former deans on the walls.

I arrived early. It was customary to bring snacks and drinks for the committee, as you want these people to be happy with you when they sit down to talk about you and your work. Nothing says "be happy" like snacks. I brought bagels, muffins, chocolate kisses, water, and Einstein Brother's coffee. I set up the table with the food nicely displayed on a platter, with plates and napkins handy, and the drinks with cups.

I brought a paper copy of my dissertation, with notes in the margins that I had reread the night before. I'd given the committee their hard copies two weeks prior as per Graduate School regulation. They had likely read it the night before as well.

My advisor, Dr. Qualitative-Research was the first to show up. It was good to see a friendly face. I was beginning to get tense and sweaty from the committee in my head reminding me of all the dire things to come. The rest of the academic committee began to file in. First, gruff Dr. Nonverbal-Communication arrived. Funny how throughout my graduate student years, other professors had told the graduate students to call them by their first names, but not him. He was dressed in his usual gray jeans and button down shirt. My stress level went up a notch upon his arrival.

He was followed by Dr. Conversation-Analysis dressed in a warm-up suit. Sad to say that at the time of my defense, he was battling colon cancer and died in December of that same year. I appreciated his coming to my meeting. He looked gaunt and frail.

Dr. Communication-and-Emotion was the other female member of my committee. She arrived in her trim black skirt and matching dark lilac cardigan and sweater set. My stress level may have declined with her arrival. She was always so kind and supportive.

Last Dr. Anthropologist came in. I'd taken several classes with him and enjoyed them. He was one of the foremost experts in his field, the Ethnography of Speaking. What was I thinking inviting someone of his caliber to be on my committee? I'm pretty sure my stress level peaked with his arrival.

Most of the committee members were in their fifties. At least I assumed they were all older than me, except Dr. Communication-and-Emotion. She was the youngest.

Once the committee was settled in those big comfy chairs, they sent me out of the room. Doing this was routine in dissertation defenses in my department. The committee members discuss the student's work without the student's presence. They decide in this conversation whether or not the research is acceptable and who is going to ask what questions. If I had been in the conference room in the departmental office, I would have had friendly staff member faces around me, who would have encouraged me and reminded me to breathe. Instead I stood in an empty corridor with the committee in my brain telling me that the people in the room beyond hated my dissertation and I was going to fail.

Finally my advisor, Dr. Qualitative-Analysis, called me back into the room. I sat at the head of that long table and readied myself for the first question. Dr. Anthropologist asked, "What makes you think this is an Ethnography of Speaking?" Uhhh… I froze. I didn't think it was. I had tried to mold it into one because at the proposal meeting, the committee thought that was the best way for me to go. Of course, Dr. Anthropologist had not been at that meeting. I fumbled some kind of answer to his question.

Faculty members in turn asked their individual list of questions about my research. I don't recall any other particular questions. I do recall that Dr. Nonverbal-Communication asked some hard questions. I actually thought of an answer to one of his questions after the meeting was over. It was a good answer too, but too late. I felt like Dr. Conversation-Analysis was just mean, which was likely his illness speaking. Dr. Communication-and-Emotion was nice, of course.

My advisor did her best to give me leading suggestions. At one point she said to me, "Don't you remember we discussed that?" Oh, yeah, I remembered and answered the question. After an hour of grilling, they thanked me and told me to wait outside again.

I went into that empty hallway and sat hunched up on the top step of a decorative stairway. With my elbows on my knees and my face in my hands, the committee in my head began to berate me. "I don't think you gave one smart answer to any question that was directed to you!" "You sounded like an idiot in there!" "I can't believe how badly that went!" I began to cry. At first it was a sniffle or two and then the tears started running down my face. I tried hard not to sob out loud. The committee in my head convinced me that I had done the worst dissertation defense in the history of defenses. All of my hard work had been for nothing.

Finally, the conference door opened. My advisor stepped out and said, "Congratulations, Dr. Corbin." What?! Did I hear correctly? *Doctor* Corbin?! Well, that turned on the tears. I was sobbing as I went back into the conference room. I sat down in a chair attempting to stop crying.

Soon everyone was up and moving out of the room. By this time, I had stifled the tears. I got hugs from Dr. Nonverbal-Communication and Dr. Conversation-Analysis. Dr. Communication-and-Emotion said, "At least you didn't cry or throw up *during* the meeting." I said,

"That happens?" She nodded. Oh my. Somehow hearing that made me feel better.

I stayed in the conference room with my advisor after everyone left. She had a list of things I needed to change in the dissertation. Thank goodness she'd kept track of what they wanted. She told me that everyone had signed the paperwork and they were not interested in seeing the changes. Wow! She gave me the signed pages that were to be submitted to the Graduate School along with the final draft of my dissertation. I could not believe it. I had been so convinced by the committee in my head that I'd failed. Then she hugged me and was off.

I had prearranged an after-dissertation-defense lunch date with my graduate school friend, Anne. She had driven more than three hours to be with me. Two months earlier, she had defended her dissertation with many of the same faculty members. Anne had been through the same thing I had just been through. She understood what it was like to face the two committees. We talked for over two hours about everything; sharing how horrible it had been for us and how miraculous it was we'd passed. I so appreciated that she had felt as stupid and unable to answer questions during her defense as I had felt. She helped me put my heart and soul back together. It had been one of the worst and most memorable days of my life, ending with the loving balm of friendship.

A SMALL GIFT STRIKES THE RIGHT CHORD
Lisa Braxton

I stood with my husband near the front of the church sanctuary, tapping my foot as the musicians played the introduction to one of my favorite tunes. On cue, we and the rest of the congregation raised our voices to accompany the band, singing the lyrics projected on two large screens.

I'd gotten to know the musicians personally. The violinist coordinated the weekly men's breakfast and operated the sound system during church service. The drummer was the facilitator of the study group I attended. The trumpeter was the bookkeeper.

I imagined myself with them at the front, hitting every note, inspiring the congregation through the ministry of song.

I shared that thought with my husband in the car on our way home that afternoon.

"Why *couldn't* you be a musician?" he said. "You could do what they're doing."

But I knew I couldn't. I was a dilettante, a dabbler, in love with the idea of being able to play an instrument but lacking the passion to put in the work. I viewed this as a shortcoming. Every time I thought about it, I felt disappointed in myself.

All the money I'm spending on lessons, it doesn't even make any sense. I remember my mother saying those words on the day of my weekly piano lesson when I was a teenager. She had good reason to complain. I'd get off the school bus, come home, and head straight for the TV room with fistfuls of Chips Ahoy cookies to eat while watching my favorite game shows. Minutes before the piano teacher pulled in front of the house, I'd open up the lesson book, thrash my way through measures, and slam down on keys with no emotion. Needless to say, my playing never improved.

Years later, after I was out of college and living on my own, I thought I was mature enough to have the discipline to practice regularly. I invested in a 61-key portable keyboard with built-in speakers and plug-in foot pedal. I hired an instructor. For about six months I practiced regularly. Then I reverted back to my old ways, practicing once a week, just before my lesson was to begin.

"You're wasting your money," the instructor snapped at me one day. We were in a tiny, windowless music room at a nearby community college. As she spoke, her voice became increasingly emotional, as if she had been holding back her thoughts for weeks. "You have to have a passion for playing music," she continued, punching the word 'passion.' "You have to want to do this. Otherwise, you'll never get anywhere with it."

She told me to think about whether or not I wanted to get serious about taking piano lessons and then get back in contact with her. I felt ashamed and embarrassed that I'd wasted her time and never called her again. I eventually sold the keyboard and did my best to tamp down any thoughts about playing an instrument.

Now in the car after church with my husband, I reminded him of my past failures. "But that was the piano," he retorted. "What about the ukulele? You should do something with that."

I'd forgotten about the little four-string instrument in its carrying case, leaning against the wall in the corner of our bedroom. It was the gift I'd chosen to get from my employer on my 10th anniversary on the job. The milestone coincided with my engagement to be married. Everything in the catalog was on my registry except for an oversized electric massage chair that wouldn't fit in the condo and a concert quality ukulele. I chose the ukulele, figuring I could continue my fantasy of becoming a musician. And that's what I did for years.

"But what if the same thing happens?" I said to my husband. "What if I slack off practicing? What if I don't like it? What if I don't have the discipline?"

"You have nothing to lose," he said. "Give it a try."

"But when would I find the time?" I persisted. "With my busy schedule, I'll never get around to practicing."

My husband began to smile as he steered the car up the drive to our condo. "You'll find the time. You've found the time for everything else."

I knew he was right. In addition to my full-time job, I took boxing and cycling classes at the gym, participated in a book club, and volunteered with a women's club. And at least three mornings a week, I squeezed in a 30-minute walk at the mall on my way to work.

I thought back on the members of the church band. They all had careers or active retirement lives along with various volunteer roles and were able to find time to practice on their instruments.

I held onto these thoughts as I walked into the music store to sign up for lessons. But my self-assuredness began to dissipate as I entered the studio. The classroom waiting area was filled with 7- and 8-year-olds accompanied by their young parents. I was in my 50s. I was sure the staff would mistake me for a grandma picking up a grandchild. When I got to the counter, I told the program coordinator that the odds were high that I would lose interest after a few lessons. She told me I could pay for lessons a month at a time and quit whenever I wanted.

I was teamed up with John, a guitarist and college student. I breezed through my first few weeks of drills and simple folk tunes, ironically because of my years of piano lessons. I got into a routine of practicing three times a week and stuck with it. John seemed thrilled with this and noted my progress each week. But playing the ukulele became more challenging once John introduced me to chords, a combination of three or more notes played together. I felt like a contortionist trying to squeeze my fingers into the right position on the strings. One of my problems was my long fingernails, which kept me from pressing down on the strings properly. John encouraged me to cut my nails. But I loved my long nails and loved to get manicures. Still, after more weeks of struggle on the instrument, I pulled out the nail clippers. My playing has improved. I increased my practice from three times a week to five times. My struggles to play chords continue, but my performance gets a little better each week.

Now I play with a ukulele group that meets once a month at a recreation center. Most of the group members have been playing for years. To my relief, there are a few novices like me. Even though I play more slowly than most and hit the wrong chord sometimes, I feel like I'm really making music. When we end a tune I have to bring myself back to reality because the music has taken me to a place of total relaxation.

Maybe I wasn't a dabbler after all, lacking the discipline for music. Maybe I just needed to find the right instrument.

THE LAMPADEDROMIA *

Sara Etgen-Baker

"Pick up the pace!" coaxed my husband.

"But I can't!" I said, my heart pounding hard inside my chest. "I can't go any faster!"

"Yes, you can! You're not fat anymore."

There it was, the *f word* and label that defined me for almost 30 years. I was born chubby, unable to shed what Mother called my natural propensity for pudginess. I became a pleasingly plump, amenable little girl, a charmingly chunky teenager, and by the time I entered college, a spirited and stout young woman. Six years later I was an obese college graduate with a promising counseling career ahead of me—a career that failed to take off.

But I was blind to my own obesity, unaware that it was at the core of my unemployability until a potential employer shared his reason for not hiring me. "Your credentials are sound, but your level of obesity tells me you have emotional issues that will diminish your effectiveness as a counselor."

His candor opened my eyes to a hard truth: I was addicted to food, having given control of my life over to it. With that realization came responsibility: I had to shed what no longer served me, confront my addiction, and prevent it and my obesity from overshadowing and defining me. Breaking my addiction was hard, requiring honest self-examination, altering my thinking patterns, and making different choices. I slowly modified my eating habits, eating only when I was physically hungry instead of when I was emotionally hungry.

Although I could barely walk down the stairs of my apartment building, I began walking to improve my mobility and awaken my all but atrophied body. Initially, I could walk for just 15 minutes at a time, my arms and legs rubbing together, chafing, and then scabbing over. But each day I pushed myself, walking five minutes longer than I did the day before, until one day I walked for an hour, and eventually two. For two years, I committed myself to healthy eating choices and maintained my walking regimen, slowly and painstakingly changing myself from being a robust, unhealthy 300-pound woman to a 130-pound healthy one. At that point, I traded my walking shoes for running shoes and became an avid runner.

My journey motivated my husband, who in March 2001 saw a commercial inviting Americans to nominate an ordinary person who inspires them to bring the Olympic flame to Salt Lake City. He nominated me to be a Torchbearer. The odds of being selected were high (210,000:1), but I was no stranger to overwhelming odds and believed my story was the stuff that would inspire others and would strike a chord with the selection committee.

Running taught me the importance of training for a race, picturing myself running a racecourse, and crossing the finish line. So for months I ran through my neighborhood carrying a broken off broom handle with a three-pound weight on it in my right hand, feeling the weight of the torch, and waving at my neighbors pretending they were cheering bystanders. I printed a picture of a Torchbearer wearing the white uniform, replaced the face with a picture of mine, taped it to my r efrigerator door, and every day visualized myself as a Torchbearer. Yes, I was in training—training to participate in an historic running event.

On September 26 while on my daily run through the neighborhood, an express package arrived. My hands trembled as I opened it and read:

"You've been selected as a *potential* support runner for the Salt Lake 2002 Olympic Torch Relay…A nationwide search was conducted for ordinary individuals who've inspired others to be both torchbearers and support runners. You've obviously touched those around you. Although all the torchbearer spots have been filled, you're eligible to be a support runner. A support runner serves as "guardian of the flame" and accompanies torchbearers carrying the Olympic Flame along its journey…Please read the attached information and return the legal forms within seven days…Congratulations!"

~

Although I wouldn't be wearing the white uniform and carrying the torch as I had imagined, I wasn't disappointed. My dream of participating in the Torch Relay was coming true! Given the odds, I was delighted to be a Support Runner and "Guardian of the Flame." I completed the required physical, submitted the forms, and waited, knowing that the letter clearly stated I was a *potential* Support Runner. Months passed without any word, but I continued my training runs through the neighborhood. Finally on December 20, another package arrived containing my official blue Support Runner uniform along with instructions on my segment of the Relay.

"Bill," I ran inside the house screaming, "I'm officially a Support Runner! We're going to Santa Fe, New Mexico!"

For the ensuing weeks and despite that winter's bitter cold, I bundled up running every day through my neighborhood, clutching my make-shift torch in my gloved hand. On January 12, my husband and I stood outside the Torch Relay collection point in Santa Fe, the cold hissing at the warmth of our bodies and licking at our faces.

"One of today's Torchbearers can't run her segment," announced the Relay organizer as she dropped folded pieces of paper into her hat. "One lucky Support Runner will become a Torchbearer. Select a number from this hat as it's passed around."

I removed my glove and reached into the hat, my numb hand trembling. I closed my eyes, stirred the contents, nabbed the first piece of paper that stuck to my fingers, and waited.

"Number 32! Who has Number 32?"

I opened my eyes and unfolded my piece of paper. "Me! Oh my God…me!"

I was whisked inside where I changed into a white Torchbearer uniform and boarded the shuttle bus with the Olympic theme song blaring over the loud speakers. The bus drove down streets lined with balloons and banners, filled with throngs of people waving American flags. At segment 32, I stepped off the bus and positioned myself to receive the flame.

The cold air, alive with spirit and excitement, took my breath away. "Hold it tightly," I thought, as the flame in the torch carried by the runner before me kissed my three-pound, icicle-shaped torch. A rush of emotion surged through my body; I turned around and ran down the street, just as I had envisioned and practiced all those months.

The very fabric of time and space unraveled; the world vanished; and I ran without my feet ever touching the ground. I waved and smiled as I floated past the bystanders; and for an instant I thought I saw Konstantinos Kondylis, the first modern-day Olympic Torchbearer, in the crowd. "The *lampadedromia* is not about you," he murmured. "It's about sharing the Olympic spirit and giving the flame of strength and inspiration to others."

Like Konstantinos, I was an ordinary person participating in an extraordinary running event—an event that had little to do with me. Yes, I was carrying the Torch; but more importantly, I was carrying the Olympic spirit. I still run, inspired to live, work, and behave with that Olympic spirit in my heart and doing my part to strengthen and inspire others.

*A *lampadedromia* is a race with lighted torches, usually a relay race, which took place in ancient Athens during rituals in honor of the deities associated with the cult of fire.

CONVERSATION

Jane Gragg Lewis

I stare at it.
This just can't be;
it's much too soon.
One. Gray. Hair.
I examine it to be sure,
but there it is, staring back at me
from her pitch-black muzzle.
My dewy eyes meet her coppery browns.
I hold her face in my hands, whisper to her,
"You can't do this to me.
You can never grow old and break my heart."
Her steady gaze whispers back,
"What the hell are you talking about?"

AGING — FOR BELLA, FOR ALL OF US

Jazz Jaeschke Kendrick

What have you lost?

For Bella, her vision — thankfully
familiarity with these rooms
fuels confidence to move about
gently bumping walls, turning
following nose to her bowls,
to her sustenance today
that she may have a tomorrow

What have you gained?

For Bella, more attention
from hovering humans —
caresses along her spine,
gentle airlifts to the counter
for medicinal tasty treats
and tolerance when out-of-box
incidents catch her by surprise

Where do you stand?

Here we all are — each of us
one day older, gaining, losing
as ground shifts beneath us —
Bella, inadvertent teacher,
models life as progression
day after day of adapting
to this, our common dilemma

Until …

LET GO, HOLD ON

Jazz Jaeschke Kendrick

Such clarity in those eyes —
blue eyes that see through, beyond
normal human perspectives —
eyes that project wisdom of
acceptance, tolerance, patience

My hope is for tenacity
to hold those blue windows
in focus as I continue beyond
trusting wisdom to find passage through
to penetrate my consciousness

The Flatlanders sing so clearly:
Life is a road stretching cradle to grave.
Each life road parallels, intersects others
collectively the planet's population evolving
losing some, gaining others, streaming onward

Though I must let go the teacher
I carry forward the lessons

TUESDAY AT MY LOCAL GROCERY STORE

Ann Haas

As soon as I enter the store, I notice shoppers jostling for motorized shopping carts. I choose a regular cart and proceed inside. Immediately, I am stopped in the veggie and fruit aisles by several seniors criss-crossed between the aisles, selecting one banana here, two potatoes there, as I try to navigate around them. I make my way to the deli aisle, where more shoppers are backed up interstate-style. It finally dawns on me that I've done it again. I've forgotten that Tuesday is senior discount day at my local grocery store and that I'll be dodging shopping carts and cost-conscious shoppers until I make my way to the checkout line.

"Hi," I say to the cashier as I'm unloading my groceries. "Long day?"

Trying to be polite, the cashier says, "Well, it's been busy today, you know, 'cause it's senior day. I'm always surprised at how many older folks show up on Tuesdays."

I shrink back a little, pondering if I should confess that I'm not really here for my senior discount but have forgotten again that it was Tuesday. I hold that thought, since I don't want her to think I'm having a "senior moment."

"One time a tour bus pulled up and unloaded 40 seniors," she continues. "Half of them turned up in my checkout line and I had to get the manager to help me keep carting back items they decided they didn't want or decided they bought too much to haul back on the bus. One of them told me they were on a special bus tour because we're the only local grocery store within a hundred-mile radius to offer a senior discount."

I shrink back a little more and keep unloading my groceries, hoisting a 12-pack of beer onto the conveyor belt.

"Excuse me," says the older gentleman in line behind me, who winks at me. "Are you old enough to drink that beer?"

I think to myself, that's the worst pick up line I've ever heard!

"Ha, ha," I respond. "I just got carded last night." He winks at me again.

"Do you remember that billboard that said: Drink Canada Dry? Well, that's what I used to do! Hardee-har-har. Yeah, I used to drink everything," he continues.

I notice people in line behind him leaning in and tittering. The cashier has stopped ringing up my purchases.

Waggling his eyebrows at me, he asks, "What time is the party at your house?"

More tittering from the folks in line, some holding up their bags of chips and waving them at me.

"Yeah, that's my favorite kind of beer." And, leering a little, "No one should drink alone," he counsels. The crowd behind him murmurs and nods.

Ok, I think, how do I get out of this one?

I hand my ID to the cashier, since this store cards everyone who buys alcohol.

"Yep," says the cashier, smiling and scanning my ID. "She's old enough – for her senior grocery discount!"

Summering after Fifty

Pat Anthony

Already autumn lurks in the ears
of corn that will be left in the field
until the whole of it turns brown
hangs upside down, dry, whispering

bluebirds and swallows line overhead wires
rocking both balance and ballet
their constant chittering foretelling
when all will wing away into
deeper forests

I want to trap the sounds, the light
the green, burgeoning prairie
but soon a total eclipse
will cover a nearby town
thousands thronging to see
some two and a half minutes of darkness

that I abhor unless sealed in sleep
shadows now some prelude
to what's coming the inevitability
of these changes ever so subtle

grasses gone to heavy heads
sunflowers turning more slowly
to follow sun moving southward

and these birds on the wire
incessantly pointing it all out.

ADVICE TO MY YOUNGER SELF
Jo Virgil

Dear Little Jo —

Let me look back on my life—the life that, I know now, will one day be yours—and tell you what I've learned.

Life is one of those journeys that comes with no map, but that's not a bad thing. That means you are just starting out to explore your own path and you get to decide when you fork to the right, when you fork to the left, when you peek behind the trees, and when you stand on top of a ridge and look down on all the beauty in front of you.

The only direction you can't go is back; the trail dissolves behind you. But you get to carry the memories and even some little keepsakes that you pick up along the way.

Oh, and a flashlight might help for the darker times, but keep in mind that it can only shine on a little spot at a time. There are no huge floodlights along the path of life, so you have to keep your main focus on where you are at the moment and on the trail directly in front of you. But even then you can only grab little glimpses of what lies ahead. And just to complicate things a bit more, the flashlight sometimes makes things appear different than they really are.

You will—literally and metaphorically—run across bluebonnets and snakes, rainbows and tornadoes, majestic oak trees and poison ivy. It's all part of the journey. Some places are scary and some places feed your soul, but a true journey needs both to really keep you alive.

Be curious. Don't take anything personally.

Remember that in many ways, life is but a dream, and you get to interpret that dream one scene at a time.

Listen more than you talk. Give more than you take.

And enjoy each moment as if it were a miracle. It is.

MARKING TIME
Nancilynn Saylor

Blessed to have known the cleansing winds
Of beauty
As well as those filled with ugliness and pain,
Remembered gusts that blew gently
Along with some that savagely roared…
Oh Youth, you were a part of them all!
Faded together, my beauties and beasts,
Truths and half-truths, and
Thinly disguised lies,
All now parts of my personal storm;
Aging just as surely as that bottle of fine German
Brandy,
A gift cherished, yet saved for
Who knows what misty-veiled future celebration.
Lately, it seems the weeks and months,
Even years
Now spin faster than my long ago children's
hamster ball.
My once dizzying treadmill slows,
Still the pages whiz from my Van Gogh calendar,
Marking another cluster
of vanished days.
The more frequent funerals of friends,
now, get-togethers to be
carefully bound in brain cells
waiting to become
remembered *Whens.*

OUR CHEE EXPERIENCE

Betsy Boyd

Mom was trying to be helpful. When I announced that I wanted to screen-in my covered deck, she offered that her next-door neighbor had had hers done by a tall, handsome Native American man, who worked very hard and did a superb job. She would get the contact information for me. "Chee!" I thought, my heart going pitty-pat.

Anyone familiar with the Tony and Anne Hillerman mysteries involving the Navajo Nation Police knows the crush-worthy Jim Chee, the sweet, smart, traditional Navajo policeman, who also trains to be a singer of curing ceremonies. The fact that he has one foot in each of two different worlds contributes much to the mystique of Jim Chee. I have a friend Cindy, who lives several states away; she and I have spent many hours hashing over the plotlines of the crimes Chee works to solve and the angst of Jim's unhappy romances. We text each other pictures of New Mexico and Arizona license plates spotted in our home states with the tag line "I saw Chee today!" We know we're acting like silly teenagers. But isn't it our playful attitudes that keep us young?

And now I would have Chee come to my home and fulfill my heart's desire to turn my deck into an outdoor oasis. The day of our appointment, I left work early to prep for having Chee evaluate my deck. I donned my best denim skirt and paired it with a colorful blouse that was set off perfectly with New Mexico turquoise earrings. Nicholas Gunn's *Grand Canyon* CD was on auto-repeat. I was excited!

But the Chee that arrived that day was not the tall, dark and handsome Navajo I'd created in my mind. Rather he was short and fair. The name on the card he handed me was Ed Sulkowski. Not only was my Chee fantasy a bust, but after Mr. Sulkowski measured my deck, he never responded to my follow-up calls and emails for his estimate. He ghosted me. Chee would never have done that!

Cindy and I share a love of New Mexico and try to meet out there every year or so, to soak in the natural beauty, history and culture of the Land of Enchantment, and, perhaps, to have a Chee encounter. Last year, while traveling across the expanse of the Navajo Reservation, we stopped in at an historic trading post mentioned in Hillerman's *The Shape Shifter*, with an eye to looking at some Navajo rugs. These typically one-of-a-kind, hand-woven rugs represent one of the most enduring art forms of the Navajo culture. They are so precious that the trading post kept them in a locked, temperature-controlled room. Our request to see some rugs was met with a gracious response from a lovely, middle-aged woman, whose long, straight dark hair was slicked back into a traditional bun. The squash blossom necklace she wore gleamed in the morning sunlight reflected through the glass storefront. Unlocking the rug room, she escorted us from stack to stack, giving us a brief education about the rugs' patterns and techniques used by the weavers. A third-generation weaver herself, she was both an expert in the art form and an excellent sales person. Like our fictional hero, she had one foot in each of two worlds, you might say. Her graciousness and patience with us knew no bounds as we considered rug after rug, taking our time to be certain of our once-in-a-lifetime selections.

Choices made, our guide escorted us to the main counter, locking the door to the rug room behind us. As she wrote up our receipts, she complimented us on our choices and explained her grandmother's method for cleaning her rugs in the snow. Because my rug was new, not a traded one, I received an 8x10-inch color photo of the weaver of my Tree-of-Life-patterned rug, as well as a card that told me a bit about the artist.

Finally, our precious new acquisitions carefully wrapped for travel and our credit card slips signed, our guide offered, "When you get home, if you have any questions about your rugs, don't hesitate to contact me," and she handed each of us a business card. The cards read:

MARY CHEE
Authentic Hand-Woven Navajo Rugs

Cindy's and my eyes met over our cards. Smiles broadened across our faces.

Sometimes the Universe gives you what you say you want, but not in exactly the form you are expecting. I did eventually find a local construction company to do my deck project, and they did a fabulous job. And that day at an ancient trading post in a remote corner of the Navajo Nation, Cindy and I finally had our Chee experience.

AGING GODDESSES

Madeline Sharples

The crones—our mothers,
    grandmothers,
aunts, old friends, and teachers—
walk arm-in-arm in pairs,
each one supporting the other
on the old cobblestone streets.
They are squat, stout
with veiny legs and thick ankles,
their bare feet in flat sandals
showing jagged toenails
or clothed in thick hose
and wide oxfords.
Some move slowly
barely able to walk,
clutching each other for support.
They are perfectly coifed.
Their hair short and bleached
hides their age
but not too much.
They wear suits
with skirts always
    below their knees.

Jeans just don't do.
They talk as they walk
closely together.
Almost in a whisper
they solve the world's problems,
impart their age-old wisdom
or decide what they'll cook for
    dinner.
They wear their age
as an example.
Softly, simply, elegantly
they are our muse.
They don't hide
but rejoice in their age.
They thrive in their togetherness.
That's what counts.
They aren't alone as they walk.
They walk together
as we follow behind.

IMPERMANENCE OF LIFE

Mary Jo West

After early morning rain,
soft, lingering mist
shrouds hillsides
of new life,
petite flowers,
the color of mustard.
By mid day,
sunlight pours over
fields bursting with
brilliant, clustered blossoms,
dressing them in
golden hues of light.
Evening shadows
cast pale over
epic display
of lavish, invasive flora.
Blossoms close
then fall,
revealing how
fleeting life is
in the natural rhythms
of a changing world.

PARADISE LOST

Linda D. Menicucci

Paradise, California, is a town in the foothills of the Sierra Nevada Mountains. Our home, and many others, are built on ridges overlooking the canyons and valleys below. Deer nibble the bushes under our windows. Squirrels chatter in trees and occasionally we see a fox, a rabbit, or a quail family scamper by. Turkeys roam the streets. Hawks dip in the sky over the canyon behind our house. Once we stopped our car to let a mountain lion pass.

This is a small community, many people were born here, many moved here to escape large cities. It is a place where life is slower, where children walk to school and people say hello to you in stores and markets. When you drive through the streets of our neighborhood, people wave. We were transplants from San Francisco and we've lived here for the past 18 years. For us, it was as close to an earthly paradise as you can find.

All that changed on November 8, 2018, when nature had its way with the town of Paradise. The temperature was about 70 degrees, almost 20 degrees above normal, a 35 to 50 mph wind was blowing, the pine trees and vegetation were bone dry after six years of drought, and the humidity was non-existent. It had not rained since May. There had been a red flag warning all week, extreme fire danger. All that was missing was a spark.

At 6:30 a.m., that spark appeared ten miles away in the area of Pulga, in the Feather River Canyon. Whipped by winds, the fire quickly spread and flew from Pulga, through the hills and valleys of Concow, and started an inferno that engulfed half of Paradise by 8:00 a.m.

25,000 people ran for their lives, as around them, flames raced up trees 60 to 100 feet high, igniting houses and melting handles and bumpers of cars. Cars ran out of gas and were abandoned, others stopped in the extreme heat blocking the way out. People ran on foot unable to breathe because the air was depleted of oxygen. The sky was black with an ominous orange underbelly; it was as black as midnight at 9 a.m.

There are three roads out of Paradise; Neal and Clark have two lanes and the Skyway has four. We were trapped in our car on Skyway as homes, businesses, pine trees, fences and telephone poles erupted around us. The traffic was stopped and everything was black. I called 911 repeatedly and got a busy signal. Finally, I got through, "Thousands of us are going to die here," I told the dispatcher and then the line went dead.

My husband looked over at me, "Call Johnny," he said, "and tell him goodbye." I tried to call our son but there was no cell service. The inferno had wiped out all communication.

It seemed we were there forever because time had stopped and then the traffic began to crawl forward. Now it was white all around us, as white as snow but it was ash. There was no visibility. I was afraid we could be rear-ended and traffic would come to a standstill, then there would be no way out. But finally, we moved. I turned to look back but I could see nothing between the ash and the black sky.

There are blanks in our memories of that morning, but we think it took us an hour and a half to drive the twenty minutes down to Chico. As the fire encroached on the town of Magalia, above Paradise, another 13,000 people joined the evacuation. Those who left at this point were trapped on the three roads out for up to six hours as the fire consumed the town and hillsides around them.

As we drove into Chico at the bottom of Skyway, we saw hundreds of people in the Raley's parking lot, many on top of their cars, looking up the Skyway toward Paradise. Many of those people were parents waiting for their children who were in school that morning. Without cell service they had no way of knowing if their children were coming out of the fire. No one was allowed to drive up to Paradise as all lanes of all roads were now headed downhill into Chico. We saw people walking the 12 miles up Skyway through the inferno to Paradise, intent on finding their families.

There are many stories of bravery, of kindness, and of duty. The firefighters who saved people in the Walgreens, who protected the hospital, the bulldozer drivers who got through to people, and firefighters who were trapped on blocked roads, the garbage man who saved an elderly woman, the school bus driver who fought the flames to save his students.

The fire roared for a month but Paradise was obliterated that day. Firefighters did all they could but it was not possible to fight a fire whipped by 50 mph winds. In the end, 15,000 homes and businesses burned. 1500 remain. As I remember the chaos of the hours of the evacuation, I am in awe that thousands of us did not die. The 86 people we lost could so easily have been 8600 in that inferno. The grace of that moment is that so many of us survived, but the future remains uncertain.

Nature will come back. It has no option. Trees will regenerate, the animals will return, growth will begin anew. The canyons and ridges we love so much will never die. Like nature, my hope is that we who live here will also regenerate, rebuilding what has become so dear, our homes, our neighborhoods, and our openness with one another. Time will tell. And time, they say, is a healer.

ACT YOUR AGE

Penelope Starr

Our cars pull into parking spaces in a lot along the Rillito River Walk every Wednesday morning at eight a.m. Sometimes all six of us show up, sometimes only two or three. One of us drives a 15-year-old Prius. Two of us are in our Honda Fits; one is gunmetal grey and the other, white. One of us has a late model sensible SUV to fit a husband's bike.

Two of us are always early and the one that hates to get up in the morning is always late. The rest of us are usually on time. We joke with the early ones saying they are OCD, feeling guilty about holding them up. Sometimes we get a last minute text – "Sorry can't make it. See you next week."

One of us covers up with long sleeves and a wide brimmed hat because she had skin cancer. She gets check-ups every six months. One of us wears very little in the Arizona summer, not even underwear, and one of us teases her about it. One of us gets cold easily so she wraps a light sweater around her hips. One of us always forgets her water bottle.

We all have grey hair but more than half of us dye it. Most of us wear prescription sunglasses. Most of us are short and getting shorter as our spines compress and osteoporosis threatens. Our average age is seventy-four.

Three of us are vigorous walkers taking the lead with long strides. One of us needs to sit on a bench or wall and rest a few times. Mostly we keep the same pace so we can talk, two or three abreast in tight rows so we can all be part of the conversation. "Don't say anything important until we go for coffee," we say because we don't want to miss anything.

Some of us have known each other for over twenty years. Two of us knew each other in our hometown. Two of us shared an art studio. One of us is a social worker and one of us makes beautiful jewelry.

We go to the cafe after our two-mile walk and two of us get cappuccinos. One has tea, one, just water. Two of us share a plain bagel. We have our frequent customer cards punched. One of us gets a free drink. We pull up chairs and crowd around a small table.

Three of us are married to men, one of us lives with a woman. One of us is moving in with her ex-husband. Three of us have mates with health challenges. We hear about their brain fog and difficulty walking and migraine headaches.

One of us has a son who is ill so we ask about him. It was a good week; he went on a road trip. Next week is chemo again. Two of us have children who live with bi-polar disorders. They are doing fine on their meds.

One of us has children living in town. The rest of us visit our children in other cities. Three of us have grandchildren; one of us has step-grandkids. We share Facebook photos on our phones.

One of us asks if we heard the story on NPR about global warming. We share our outrage at the idiotic things our elected officials say. One of us says she heard a story about the fallibility of contraceptives and we agree that we are glad to be past all that.

One of us is afraid of taking a general anesthetic for a colonoscopy and asks for advice. The rest of us reassure her that it's a type of twilight sleep and she will be fine. We tell her our doctors' names and say we will email them to her. One of us had a frozen shoulder and she praises her physical therapist for helping her avoid surgery. One of us needs another knee replacement. We laugh about having replacement parts.

One of us has parents in their nineties in an assisted living facility. Her father has a number of life-threatening conditions and her mother's anxiety and bossiness is making it worse. Two of us had difficult mothers and can empathize. One of us feels lucky that her father died at eighty-seven without a prolonged illness. She misses him every day.

One of us has a cough. Three of us offer her advice. Get an inhaler. Don't eat dairy. Go to an ear-nose-throat doctor. One of us says she is worried about the cougher; it's been a long time with no relief.

One of us is going on an Elderhostel trip to Greece. One of us just returned from presenting a workshop at a conference in Kansas City. One of us is going to Maine to sell her house. One of us says take Airborne before flying to prevent getting a cold on the plane.

Two of us get up to go to the bathroom. When they return, two more go.

One of us has to go to work so she says goodbye. Two of us say we have to go to the grocery store on the way home. One of us is going shopping for a dress to wear for her fortieth wedding anniversary party.

One of us says that the elderly man at the next table who is pretending to read is really listening to our conversation. We recap what we have discussed: vaginal plastic surgery, Black Lives Matter and white people, global warming, mates who need a lot of guidance in the grocery store, the pros and cons of Hillbilly Elegy and constipation remedies.

One of us announces the time. We get up to go. One of us has trouble with a stiff hip and hobbles over to put her cup in the bussing bin. One of us can't find her sunglasses and one of us says they are on the table. Someone says getting older isn't for sissies.

We say goodbye to the eavesdropper who acts surprised. One of us says we know you were listening to our conversation. We'll be back next week.

We go outside, hug goodbye, and laugh about the earful he got. That's what older women talk about – everything.

ROLE REVERSAL

Betsy Boyd

I was worried. It was two days after my 85-year-old father lost his balance, falling backwards in his driveway and hitting his rear-end and head on the concrete. Tests run at the emergency room that night showed no damage to his head, neck, shoulders, and spine, but they did reveal something suspicious going on in his right kidney. We were at the hospital again for additional testing. While the emergency room CT scan revealed no new damage, it could not have detected the problem that was creating such bewilderment for him on this particular trip to the hospital—Alzheimer's.

We were late for our appointment, made later because the parking lot was largely full and we had to park in the farthest row from the door. Stressed on so many levels, I was attempting to rush Dad along when I noticed out of the corner of my eye that he stubbed the toe of his right shoe, which caused him to stumble a bit as he caught his balance. A few steps later, it happened again. It was at that moment that I flashed back 61 years to a similar scene.

I was five. My mother always said that if you do something you're not supposed to, something always happens, and that day it did. I had been told that I could go to the neighborhood playground but not to swing on the swing because the chain was broken. To my delight, when I arrived at the playground, I saw that the chain was fixed! Someone had cleverly tied the broken, rusty chain into a knot. It made one side of the swing shorter than the other, but that was a minor detail. I reeee-ally wanted to swing, and I couldn't see any reason why I shouldn't. Up I went! Up, up, higher and higher I soared in my lopsided seat… until suddenly I felt it give way, while I continued soaring through the air. Before I knew what was happening, I hit the ground with a thud, bending my right wrist backward. The shooting pain in my wrist was exceeded only by the dread of having to tell my mom I had disobeyed her and hurt myself.

Dad had to be called from work to come pick me up and take me to the hospital, while Mom stayed home with my younger sister and baby brother. He was worried; his little girl was hurt. He needed to get back to work as soon as possible. He had a tense grip on my arm, holding it high above my head as we silently made our way to the ER door. I had to scramble across the parking lot, taking four quick steps to his one. So there we were, Dad taking his long, hurried strides and me doing my best to scurry along beside him.

"Why doesn't he slow down?" I remember thinking. "Doesn't he know I'm just a little girl?"

Sixty years melted away in the split second it took my brain to process this memory and for the irony of the current moment to wash over me.

I slowed down to match Dad's pace. He didn't stumble again the rest of the way to the check-in desk.

LAVENDER DREAMS

Marjorie Witt

As the springtime rains slowly converge into our dry California summer, I realize that we have not tended our front yard in the last three years since we returned to living at the house. I get a sudden urge to rake, weed, and clean up areas where the kitties had created smelly piles of outdoor litter boxes. After cutting back the blackberry bushes across the front, I find two sage plants my younger son had left behind are still there and fairly healthy. I remove the chicken wire surrounding an unidentifiable bush, now a mere skeleton the deer left behind.

It has always been a hit-or-miss endeavor to find what grows in our clay soil hillside, survives turkeys, raccoons and deer, let alone lack of water, trimming and tending. Over the years, we gradually gave in and let nature take over with a backdrop of blackberries, poison oak, pyracantha, and ivy.

The trouble is, the yard looks barren once I clean it up. The pea gravel that we had used as a ground cover during the last drought is thinning. Bits of the plastic rolls we had placed under the rocks as weed prevention wave in the summer breeze. I decide against ordering another truckload of pea gravel and instead push the rocks around to create several bald areas for new plants. Since the sage is doing well, I figure maybe a little lavender might thrive. They seem like the same variety of plant to me and I have always liked lavender. Somewhere I heard that cats don't like lavender, so it seems an ideal solution to make the yard smell better.

Lavender plants are on sale this week. I never realized there is more than one type of lavender, however, and confronted with a decision-making process, I opt for the easiest way out. I bring home one of each.

Having visions of purple hillside bliss, or maybe even a beautiful English garden, I move the plants around to several locations, raking rocks back and forth trying to figure out the best layout. I try to appreciate a Zen moment here and there until I figure out my mind doesn't work in a mindful manner. This task is way beyond any gardening skills I could ever achieve. I think back to when we were first married, over forty years ago and that Japanese gardener my husband had hired. We had a perfectly mowed and trimmed lawn and plush ivy in the front yard and the backyard was developing into a well thought out landscape of ice plant and juniper with a dash of colorful plants that I could never name. Heck, I could never tell the difference between a daisy and a sunflower. I should never have fired him.

By the time I figure out the most suitable spots for the lavender, it is near time for Grandpa and Little J to return from their "escape from Grandma for a day" outing. I'll just get the shovel and be done with this, I think. Finding the shovel is another ordeal. It isn't where I had found the rake, tossed aside in the pool yard. It isn't with the yard brooms on the back patio. It isn't up on the hillside as far as I can see. I look at the flat-sided shovel I had used to remove some nature-made kitty litter. No way is that going to dig into the hardening clay soil. I must go to the store again. I set the plants aside. Another day. Yes, it will have to happen on another day.

A week later, I find the time for the next excursion to the nursery. This time I have seven-year-old Little J in tow. "I'll let you pick some plants. You can have your own little garden, JJ," I try to convince him as he argues that he would be much happier with a trip to the local toy store. Finding the shovel is no problem. Finding Little J is a problem. He decides the nursery is a perfect place for a little hide and seek. It takes less than two minutes to find him. In the meantime, I determine that he must have been kidnapped by a Lego-bearing bearded old Santa man and is halfway to the Nevada desert by now. Then I hear the crash. Fortunately for my budget, he has only dropped a tiny little ceramic elf creature, and the clerk assures me it wasn't his fault. "We shouldn't have had that on the other side of the cacti. I hope he didn't get stuck too badly by those thorns. It's OK. You don't have to pay for it."

All right, so she doesn't want to get sued for leaving dangerous boy-eating plants within a child's reach. Feeling obligated now to spend more money, we leave with $46 worth of cacti and a $10 shovel. It could have been more expensive. Little J had begged for a big ugly bright green pot with toads hanging over the edge. I convinced him we had a suitable pot at home, describing it to him as a huge brown cactus pot that his daddy used to have. I didn't tell him I found it in the back of his daddy's closet under the grow light of a healthy three-foot-tall pot plant. Little J is still trying to suck the prickles out of his thumb as I load the trunk.

We can't find the huge pot when we return home. It is then I remember that Big J had retrieved that pot on one of his recent visits. It takes a while, but I get Little J to agree that I can plant his cacti in two smaller pots and that way he could have two gardens. Notice, *I* plant the cacti. Little J is still nursing the thumb that now resembles one of his new prize plants, swollen and prickly. We set the lavender aside for another day and head for the tweezers.

I keep a close eye on the shovel and lavender hoping neither will disappear before I complete my landscape plan, which ends up happening a week later. By now, the larger of the plants is looking bedraggled but I am sure it will perk up once it settles into its new home. I dig a hole twice as big as the root ball. Somewhere I had read to do that. I fill it with potting soil that I found in the back of the storage shed, figuring it had grown a good crop of pot so most likely would work well in my endeavors, too. As I tamp down the surrounding dirt, I feel satisfied that I have completed a job well done. The small plant looks a little healthier and I stick it in the yard in haste. After a little more rearranging of rocks and a good watering, I think the yard looks darn good. Not like the Zen garden on my smartphone, but it is a start.

Two weeks later, my friend Pat arrives to pick me up for our ladies' luncheon. Relieved that she doesn't ask to use my bathroom, knowing my house inside is a big disaster, I ask if she would like to see my front yard. She had been in my house before and I figure it is a safe assumption that she doesn't want to enter that den of cat-scented chaos any more than I want to explain why I still haven't ousted the six cats that have taken up residence (another long story). "Sure," she says. "Let's look." Rounding the corner, the first thing I see is a huge pile of dog poop, right next to the now dried up, gray, and nearly naked lavender twigs. Seeing the dismay on my face, Pat diplomatically says, "I think maybe it's not quite the right environment."

I take a moment to recover. "I think we're running late," I say. We get into the car, and as Pat backs her way down the long steep driveway, I'm thinking, *take me away.... I feel like a dried-up old lavender.*

DINNER WITH THE BUTTERFLY WHISPERER

Sara Etgen-Baker

I entered Whispering Oaks, where I found the large French doors of the dayroom flung wide open; the August air—light and fresh—gently blew the long, crisp, white curtains to and fro. I walked through the doors toward the verandah and saw Pop sitting outdoors amongst some zinnias surrounded by a rabble of butterflies.

He was slumped over in his wheelchair, his limp left arm tied to the chair's railing. He looked up and waved with his good hand. "Sara!" he called with delight. My breath caught in my throat and I choked back the tears. I closed my eyes and felt the pull of childhood memories urging me to leave.

You can't turn back; he needs to see you, reminded the voice inside my head.

But I can't bear seeing him like this. It's hard.

Yes, it's hard, but he needs to see you. So, you must be brave. Be brave for him, the voice answered, firm as a rock. *Don't turn back. Not now.*

I opened my eyes; a mixture of sunlight and shadow filtered through the large oak trees casting a warm honeyed tone along the narrow footpath in front of me.

Remember, continued the voice, *don't let him see you sad or upset. He needs your strength.* I swallowed hard, squared my shoulders, and meandered my way along the footpath toward Pop, my legs unsteady beneath me.

I sat down next to him and laid our lunch on the picnic table in front of Pop. "Da…da…dinner for ta…ta…two!" He flashed me an impish grin. "Re…re…remember?"

"Yes, Pop! I sure do!" I leaned toward him and gave him a kiss and big hug. "Summer afternoons, we'd sit together at the picnic table in our backyard, eating burgers and drinking chocolate milkshakes while we watched the butterflies dance around Mother's zinnias."

"Ya…ya…yes." He nibbled on his burger and sucked on the straw as best he could, taking short drinks of his chocolate shake. "Sooooo ga…ga…good! La…la…love you!"

"Love you, too, Pop." I squeezed his right hand and took a long drink of my own milkshake. Minutes passed by, and a little blue butterfly landed on my nose. Then a big yellow butterfly gently floated over and landed on Pop's shoulder. Soon a kaleidoscope of them floated up and down around him like a swirl of multicolored petals. I watched in awe and remembered when butterflies swarmed around him in our backyard; for most of my youth, I truly believed Pop possessed some type of magical ability that attracted butterflies. Later, though, I convinced myself he didn't necessarily possess magical butterfly powers, believing instead that Pop simply made them feel welcome and safe. Regardless of the reason, the butterflies gravitated toward him like iron shavings to a magnet. There was no denying it; he was then and was still *the butterfly whisperer*.

Time passed imperceptibly as we continued eating our burgers and watching the butterflies flutter from flower to flower. Occasionally one of them landed on the stem of a flower that had already passed its peak, its petals blackened at the edges and curling. It folded its wings neatly upward and partook of the flower's nectar, seemingly unaware that summer would quickly become fall, that the leaves would soon tumble, and that the nights would close in, chilly and long. The butterflies and flowers continued dancing together as one, living in the moment without a single thought about the future or the past.

I, on the other hand, drifted back to those summer days when I found myself in Pop's company. On one such day, Pop discovered me sitting at our picnic table crying over the fates of the butterflies in our backyard.

"They only live a few days," my lips quivered around the words.

"My darling daughter. Nothing lasts forever, but you needn't be sad for the butterflies; they live a beautiful life," he said in a comforting voice. "Remember, the butterfly counts not months but moments. So, it has enough time." He then went inside the house, made us chocolate milkshakes, and returned to the picnic table, where we drank in silence relishing the butterflies that flittered around Mother's zinnias.

On another summer day, Pop drove me to a wooded area near our home for the sole purpose of capturing butterflies. "Once you spot a butterfly, approach it slowly so as not to startle it." He handed me a butterfly net, demonstrating how to sweep the net forward, flip it over the handle, and flatten the net bag so the butterfly's wings closed. "Now, using your other thumb and forefinger, reach into the net and grasp all four wings and remove the butterfly."

I followed his instructions, eventually netting a giant swallowtail butterfly. "Now, whisper a wish and let it go."

"Let it go? Seriously!? What's the point in capturing it in the first place?"

"According to Native American folklore, if you want a wish to come true, you must first capture a butterfly and whisper your wish to it. And since the butterfly makes no sound, it cannot tell your wish to anyone but the Great Spirit who hears and sees all. As thanks for giving the butterfly its freedom, the Great Spirit always grants the wish." Pop winked at me and smiled. "So, whisper your wish and let the butterfly go."

Pop squeezed my hand, jolting me back to the present. "La…la…love you."

"Love you too, Pop!" I kissed him on the cheek. "Look, Pop!" I pretended to capture a butterfly between my thumb and forefinger. "I caught a butterfly!"

"Wh…Wh…Whisper." His eyes sparkled, vibrant as ever; but when he tried to wink, he couldn't. "Ma…ma…make wa…wa…wish," he said, his words disjointed.

Watching Pop try to wink or talk was more than my heart could handle; so I closed my eyes and whispered, "Oh Great Spirit, erase the stroke and make my father whole again." But no amount of wishing would ever make my father whole again.

"I…I…had enough time," Pop clasped my hand. "Da…da…don't wo…wo…worry. I be free soon. Bu…bu…but I not a…a…afraid. I…I…ready to go." A single tear dropped from his eye. "Uh…uh… understand?"

"Yes, Pop," my chin trembled. "I understand." Although I understood, I just couldn't bear the thought of losing him. But like the butterflies I'd loved as a child, I knew he'd be gone soon—sooner than I wanted. "Oh, Pop," I gulped hard. "You have the grace and soul of a butterfly. I love you."

Throughout the remainder of summer, Pop and I continued watching butterflies outside the verandah. But I could not keep summer with us forever, nor could I halt the changing season. The flowers on the verandah withered; the leaves tumbled and rustled about; and the nights eventually closed in, chilly and long. And one-by-one the butterflies vacated the flowers on the verandah and began their annual migration southward. Pop, too, vacated the verandah and began his own migration of sorts. And in that moment of loss, my world collapsed; and my heart broke into a thousand pieces.

Years have come and gone since Pop's passing. Although the pain of losing him has diminished, I still miss Pop and sitting with him at our picnic table, sharing a milkshake on a warm summer afternoon, and watching the butterflies flitter around Mother's zinnias. That picnic table now sits in my own backyard. I frequent it during the warm summer months, indulging myself in a milkshake and watching the butterflies dance around the zinnias my husband planted. Although they don't gravitate toward me like they did Pop, a single butterfly occasionally lands next to me. I'd like to believe it's Pop sitting next to me, and we're once again eating burgers, drinking milkshakes, and sharing dinner together at our very own table for two.

WHEN I AM EIGHTY

Jeanne Zeeb-Schecter

My late mother-in-law, Eva, used to say, "When I am eighty maybe then I will be a grown-up, maybe then I will know everything." Eva was my guru. We would regularly sit across from each other at her dining room table and share a pot of English Breakfast tea or a glass of scotch, depending on the time of the day, talking about the day's good and bad, and she dispensed her hard-won wisdom to me.

Her golden nuggets of insight usually started with a tongue-twisting Yiddish saying like, "A mentsh trakht un got lakht." She would then translate into English, "Man plans and God laughs," followed by a short explanation like, "We think we know what will happen and make plans for it, but only God knows how it will really go down."

Another gem along the same lines was, "Make your plans with a pencil." I learned that life took many twists and turns, and things rarely go exactly the way we plan. So, have a pencil with an eraser and learn to adapt. She taught me that aging brings changes and we have to accept and go with those things that can't be changed. The times I've thought about and implemented her wisdom during the past thirty-four years are too numerous to count.

Eva had the right to dole out this wisdom. She was never a Pollyanna. At birth, one of her eyes was damaged by forceps, leaving her with sight in just the one eye. She was also born without her right hip socket. In the 1920s, all the doctors knew was to place her into a hard body cast for many months in Children's Hospital. She was separated from her family during that time because her parents had to enlist government funds, making her a temporary ward of the court. They weren't allowed into her hospital room, adding to the trauma. However, her hip remained deformed and she walked with a pronounced limp for her entire life. When at eighteen she began to work, she was finally able to buy an eye case, so that her eyes looked the same. But, with all that, she never became a victim and was determined to have a normal life. She worked in a doctor's office, married the perfect man, and was able to have two children delivered by C-section. She was only five feet and one inch tall, but she was a giant in courage and bravery.

She met aging the same way, head on, never giving up on learning new things and adapting to changes. As she and Papa needed more help, they moved closer to us so that her son and I could do more for them. We helped them find a beautiful Senior Living apartment building close by. At first she said, "There are only old people here." But she immediately began to cultivate women friends, who became sisters to her. She laughed with them and, when her husband died a few years later, they all cried together. Her "sisters" helped to soothe her pain and re-enter a different life.

She stepped up her volunteer work at the nearby St. Joseph's Hospital and played Bingo three times a week. She used an Access van to visit friends all around the Los Angeles area and go to a monthly Yiddish club, where she could maintain the language she grew up with at home. In her own way, she was adventurous. She loved and enjoyed her three grandchildren, watching them grow into special adults. Twice a year she flew to upstate Minnesota to be with her daughter and son-in-law and his family. My husband and I spent many evenings and holidays with her. She took my two children and grandchildren from my first marriage into her heart, as she had done with me. She would tell me, "There's always enough love for everyone."

Eva taught me that aging is a double-edged sword. On one side you are alive and blessed enough to be here and watch your family grow. Life is a miracle. On the other side, we lose loved ones and family as we outlive them, and that is painful. She showed me that life is usually balanced, even though you might not see it at the time. Eva and my husband were my constant comfort when I lost my son in 1995 after a three-year battle with AIDs. I spent many afternoons, after closing my office, at her table, letting her wisdom and comfort seep into the deepest parts of my heart, laughing and crying with her.

Today, years after she died, I am the retired seventy-five-year-old, in the winter of my life. But, because she was in my life, I am finding new adventures that keep me fully engaged in this season. I have joined three writing groups and now teach a Creative Life Writing class myself. I am writing a book. I joined Story Circle three years ago. I have great-grandchildren that keep me young and laughing because their joy and wonder is contagious. I get up off the floor much slower than I used to, but that is a small price to pay for helping to string dinosaurs on a hand laundry line with little Michael, so that his T-Rex, stegosaurus, and brontosaurus can "fly." My oldest at fourteen thanked me for giving him "life advice" in my birthday card this year. Although I didn't give it in Yiddish, I am paying it forward for Eva. I have things to share with my husband at the end of each day because I stay busy, creative, and content.

I have purposively created special bonds with several women in my writing classes and we laugh together and cry together over lunches and visits. We comfort and bolster each other when it's needed. We congratulate each other's successes. We regularly affirm our sisterhood as unique and special.

At seventy-five, I am still learning how to do this thing called Life, which is always changing. I keep a pencil with an eraser at my side and maybe, just maybe, when I'm eighty, I will be a grown-up.

SCALLOPS
Juliana Lightle

I want to open my eyes
wide, unblinking
I want to face the
cold granite truth
I want to pry open
deceptions, like
scallops white, vulnerable
I want to stand

cup my ears to hear
ancient voices
I want to walk
empty spaces
where mind and beauty join

I want to bravely
walk toward death
arms wide open, welcoming.

AWAKENED SENSES
Susan Flemr

Dear Mother,

On a crisp October day in your 98th year, we took our final walk outdoors.

As I wheeled you onto the nursing home patio, I watched the sun cover your snowy hair. "Oh, Mom! Do you feel that sun? It is only 65 degrees today, but it feels so much warmer, don't you think?" You gradually raised your head and responded, "Yes, it does, Susie."

I remembered… You and I walked hand-in-hand as I faced a new life experience. You squeezed my hand and said, "Oh, Susie! Do you feel how wonderfully warm the sun is today? I think you are going to have a happy first day of kindergarten. Let's skip a little bit, shall we?"

I moved your chair to a garden walkway. "Mom, look at the marigolds, zinnias, and all the Fall flowers." You reached out to touch the bright gold, orange, and red blossoms at your side as you spoke, "Oh, I do so love them. Do you know October is my favorite month? I met your Daddy in October of 1934." I chuckled and said, "Oh, I thought you were going to say it was because I was born in October." You said, "Oh, that too!" We laughed together.

I remembered… "Susie, just look at the leaves. How many colors can you find? Soon they will cover the ground and it will be fun to rake them up and jump in them. Oh, Susie, I remember walking through crunchy leaves the night before you were born. Your Daddy was away with the Marines getting ready to ship out to the Pacific. I missed him so. But then you arrived amid all the bright fall colors and life was better."

We moved to a group of empty lawn chairs where I sat next to you and asked, "Do you feel the breeze out here? It has been a while since you have been outside." Again, you raised your head and closed your eyes before you finally answered, "Oh, yes! I can feel that breeze and it feels so good."

I remembered… "Come down here, Susie. You can feel the breeze coming across the lake. I think it might be bringing some rain tomorrow. Oh, this is such a relief from the summer heat, isn't it?"

A cardinal in a nearby tree announced his presence. You didn't seem to notice the bird, so I asked, "Can you hear the cardinal sing?" You laughed, "Yes, I remembered to put in my hearing aids. I love that call."

I remembered… "Let's stop chattering for a few minutes, Susie. Just stand still and use your ears. I think that is a robin we hear, and a little chickadee too."

Your eyes remained closed. "Mom, would you like a drink of water?" You opened your eyes, reached for the bottle, sipped, and handed it back. "Oh, thank you. It is so refreshing."

I remembered… Dad pulled the family car up to a roadside fruit stand. You leaped from the car and bought a bag of Bing cherries. After you returned to the car, and pulled out a handful of cherries for you and Dad, you handed the bag to us in the back seat and instructed us, "Don't miss the sweet burst of taste, kids. There's nothing better."

"Can you smell that, Mom? It seems like someone is burning leaves." You breathed in deeply, "Yes! Now I smell it. Oh, glorious Fall."

I remembered… "Now before any of you run off to the cabin, I want you to stop right now and take a deep breath through your nose. Those grand tall pine trees are already giving us a beautiful gift that we will enjoy all week before we head back to the city, kids. Oh, isn't that wonderful?"

The afternoon sun slipped down behind the tree line and your chin dropped to your chest as you dozed. I wheeled you back into the building and down the hall to your room. As I helped you into your favorite chair, you hung onto me, we hugged, and you said, "Thank you, Susie, I needed that." I replied, "I needed that, too, Mother."

You reached up and touched my cheek, "I do so like it when you call me 'Mother.' That was what you called me when you were young." I assured you, "I will do that from now on."

As I walked toward the door, you called me back. "I could use one more hug, Susie." I returned and wrapped you in a long hug. You laughed and said, I am glad you have your Daddy's long arms."

And now, dear Mother, I am in my 76th year of life. I sit by an open window in a North Woods cabin. I feel the breeze off the nearby lake, I smell the grand tall pines pour out their gift to me before I return to the city, and I listen daily to the beloved heart-wrenching wail of the loon.

I am grateful for the lessons you taught me so many years ago. You awakened my senses…taught me how to look, to sniff, to listen, to touch, to taste, to stand in awe of the earth…and to share love. Thank you, Mother.

GIVE ME A HEAD WITH HAIR...
LONG, BEAUTIFUL HAIR

Bonnie Watkins

Hair. I didn't have much to speak of for the first two years of my life. Mama used to glue a tiny pink bow in the wisps atop my head with a dot of white paste made from flour and water. Guess that the pink frilly dresses and lace trimmed socks still didn't broadcast loudly enough that I was a girl.

Fast forward to the vicious gossipy halls of junior high and high school in the late 1960s, where having naturally curly hair in an era of straight hair fashion promised a definite liability. I tried synthetic straighteners that my African-American friends used, but they made my hair fall out.

Then I read about rolling your hair on empty orange juice cans, the giant cardboard kind that held frozen Minute Maid orange juice concentrate. These required all manner of bobby pins, long metal clips, short metal clips...tried them all. Still, the cans posed a serious balancing act feat and didn't really straighten much.

Drugstore shelves and salons didn't yield the impressive array of hair products that they do today. In fact, one of the very first came out in my day and was all the rage: Dippety-Do. The glass jar revealed beautiful aqua gel with pretty pockets of air bubbles. It was pretty expensive for the day, but my pocketbook had to expand because the need was great. So great that it took about half a jar to make my hair an iron helmet. Slicked against the sides of my hair were single curls around the ears (My ears developed first and until the rest of my body caught up, they were rather large, the subject of taunts, and thus had to be covered.) To keep those curls flat, I scotch-taped them to my cheek. This wasn't just every third day when I washed and styled my hair with Dippety-Do, but each non-wash night: a dab of gel around the curl and another piece of tape. This took a toll on my cheek skin, but hey, what price beauty, especially for a teenaged girl.

Next I tried another fad of the day: ironing my hair to straighten it, before the days of flat iron appliances. For my pains, I got a slightly scorched ear and, once again, not very straight hair. It didn't help that

I lived on a small dairy farm about 30 miles west of Houston, with plenty of hot, messy outside work that I was both expected to but also happy to share with my dad, who ran everything alone without other help. Ever-present humidity popped those natural curls right out.

Senior year followed with high hair requirements. The up-do dominated senior proms of the era. To my collection of hair attachments, I added a shorter hairpiece for height. Off to the stylist for prom night. Although neon-colored hair wasn't popular then, my hair could have rivaled *The Simpson's* TV series mom Marge's high, blue hair. And, the stylist carefully adorned my impressive tower of hair with cascading fabric daises that matched the yellow voile overlay of my long gown with the same daises sprinkled down one side.

My next hair challenge was upcoming graduation. My graduation cap looked goofy without lots of hair beneath it and my natural hair then was shorter, which didn't help pull out the curls, but patient reader, you can see how I had tried potions, unguents, and techniques, and nothing had helped. So next came the purchase of what was then called a fall. This was a long straight length of synthetic hair that would fall straight down the back, hence the name. Procedure: comb natural hair back and then insert the attached large, curved comb at the top of the head. To hide the line of demarcation, a headband was necessary. For the dance after prom, I purchased every color and variety: lacey, velvet, corduroy; you name it, I had it. However, if I really got wound up on the dance floor after prom to Chubby Checker's "Twist and Shout," the fear that the fall might literally fall right off my head loomed, thus making the wig truly live up to its name.

The University of Texas freed me in many ways: ideas, attitudes, lifestyles, and hair! Free to let my freak flag fly, longer, unkempt curls blowing in the wind helping to solidify the motto of Texas' capital city long before it became a bumper sticker: KEEP AUSTIN WEIRD.

Fast-forward again to later mothering years where even time to brush your hair in the morning constituted a legitimate check on the daily list of accomplishments. The long curls stayed and the babies loved to anchor themselves by holding on to them for security. No fashion judgment either from nonspeaking babies!

Hold that fast forward button several decades to grandparenting years, when grandchildren who can speak verify the quotation by Oliver Wendell Holmes, Sr., "Pretty much all the honest truth telling there is in the world is done by children." One night, lying beside my four-year-old grandson in bed, happily reading through the large stack of books to postpone bedtime, I felt his fingers in my hair, twirling it. "Nonnie, your hair is weird. It just curls and twirls all around and crazy everywhere." My subsequent genetics lesson, following the family tree for those who inherited curly hair, as his mom and I had, and those who inherited straight hair, as his dad and he had, fell on deaf ears. But he was happy twirling and I was happy being near him, being twirled.

Truth also be told honestly now by the eternal child in me as I have grown older: I have wondered not where all the flowers have gone, but where all my hair has gone! But growing older hopefully brings more wisdom. When I finally gave up the tyranny of style and the pettiness of popularity so important in high school, and surrendered to those thick, black curls that served me well through university, motherhood, and decades beyond, freedom reigned. Gratitude came when I let my freak flag fly then, and I am grateful now for my come-full-circle-not much-hair, now silver, but still uniquely weird and twirly.

HOMAGE TO MY BREASTS
Maya Lazarus

These breasts are a hand-full
no more, no less. Once perky,
now weighed down by age
these nipples will not
surrender.

They stand at attention
through cold and heat.
Through layers of clothes
they poke out, still to be seen.

These breasts have benefited
the mouths of my two children.
They have taken me
    to the precipice
of enjoyment, the ecstasy
of contentment, fondled and held
lovingly by men.

These breasts no longer wish
to be restrained. They hang free
like ripe mangoes
on a strong, steady branch.

THINGS I'VE THOUGHT ABOUT
Carol J. Wechsler Blatter, LCSW, DCSW

I couldn't see
   spring's budding flowers
I couldn't see rabbits
   foraging for food
I couldn't see people gathering
I couldn't see anything.

She went into a coma,
her brain bled.
She wasn't suppose to die,
I didn't authorize it.
Who authorized it?
God?

Should she be mad at God,
burdened burying her son
before her own death?
Maybe he took his own life?
A child should bury a parent,
never should a parent bury
her child.

Maybe a tree?
Did you see it?
I planted one once.
It died in an ice storm.

People die.
You know,
famous ones make
news,
their bodies seen by hundreds.
No one sees a homeless body,
It's just another body.

When I die, yes, I will die
sitting here in this chair,
just when I'm ready to sip coffee
from the mug you once gave me.

FINDING MY ROOTS: GROWING OLDER
Jo Virgil

I have spent a lot of time in my life, especially in the past several years, trying to find my roots—and I don't mean genealogy. I mean my own self, my purpose, the factors of my life that ground me and help me to grow, like roots do for trees. But that may not be an appropriate metaphor. I have never wanted to be literally grounded, stuck in one place without change, without exploration—and even that description I mean both literally and metaphorically.

Maybe I'm looking for roots that move with me, roots that can be transplanted without trauma. But then, is that really what a root is? Don't roots aim for stability? But it could be true that roots also aim for growth—not just for themselves, but also to encourage and support the plant they represent, the plant they feed and stabilize, the plant they are part of.

So, what roots am I seeking? Maybe a skill or a talent that I want to nurture? Maybe a spiritual path that helps me branch out into the unknown? Maybe a dive into the meaning of my life, or the meaning of life overall?

I've always had a deep-seated need (or, to keep in line with the metaphor, a "deep-seeded" need) to belong, to be important to someone, or to a group or a community or a tribe. But I've also always felt a need to be unique, independent, untethered. So what kind of root can match both of these goals?

That's a tough question—and maybe that explains why this quest for finding my roots has been such a challenge. Maybe I'd rather not have roots.

Maybe I'd rather fly like an eagle.

ANTI-AGING CREAM
Madeline Sharples

That's great stuff
if you're young.
Maybe it will help
keep your wrinkles away
at least for a few more years.
But if you wait too long,
don't bother.
Those wrinkles are fixed
in your skin like cement.
No amount of heavy
or light or oily cream
no matter what it costs

will budge them
off your face.
So stop hoping,
stop kidding yourself,
stop wasting your money.
You're better off
sitting in the dark,
maybe in a movie theater,
so no one can take a look at
the aging woman
you've already become.

AGING

Juliana Lightle

"Rage, rage against the dying of the light."
— *Dylan Thomas*

Custom says, "Age gracefully."
Are they crazy, dumb?

Who wants to look
old
wrinkled
grey?

They lie!
All of them.

Who wants a broken mind
confused
unfocused
lost?

Shoot me!
Burn my bones.
Scatter them
in the desert sands
to feed
desert willow where
rattlesnakes lie
searching for shade.

CARPE DIEM, OLD FRIEND
Sarah Fine

There comes a time when the firmness of a mattress is more important than the person with whom you share the bed. Is this the end to romance or a natural progression in the aging dance? You don't love the mattress in the same way you love your partner. You don't actually 'love' the mattress at all, but you need the mattress to be firm.

At some point in the past and likely in the future, you will need that partner more than a mattress. So this may not be a thought you want to share. But it is a thought that brings me to the topic of aging.

As I age, I don't feel different inside except in the positive ways you experience when you feel 'older and wiser.' It did get better. I can recall though faintly now the angst of my youth, the struggles of my working life, the downward spirals of my romances, and the self doubts of my parenting years.

It did get better. At this moment in time, my three children all have jobs and are generally happy. They still have things to accomplish but they are on a road of their own choosing and they are blessed with good health.

The Beatles song "Will you still need me, will you still feed me, when I'm 64?" has come and gone. I find I am still needed, though maybe not as often, by my family, my friends, and my community. I am grateful to have no worries about a lack of food or money, though I am regrettably past the time when I can eat whatever I want whenever I want.

"Can you imagine us years from today, sharing a park bench quietly? How terribly strange to be seventy." Now my 70th birthday has come and gone, too. I am post that Paul Simon song and wondering why he thought 70 was so old—though I do remember agreeing with him when I was 21.

Some of my old friends are gone already. They didn't get to be 70 and I am learning to live with that. It's one of the inevitabilities of aging. You become the older generation. Your parents die and then your dearest friends. You make new friends but it's different. It's a selfish thought but there's no one around now who knew me when….

In 1964, I attended a Beatles concert at Maple Leaf Gardens in Toronto, which was not a garden at all but rather the place where our city hockey team played. I was 17 years old and a big fan of the Beatles, but not the screaming or fainting kind.

Last year at Doreen's memorial service, I was reminded how she lined up at the Gardens overnight to get $5 tickets for the many of us who were not allowed to be out that late. I hope we were grateful. Doreen died a few months before her 70th birthday.

Her favourite Beatle was Ringo. Mine was John. My best friend Margaret's was Paul. I remember the concert and the fans screaming. I was singing along with the band and Margaret hushed me. I laughed because I didn't think my singing could ever compete with all that screaming.

Margaret, who was always the one I imagined sharing that bench with in our old age, died in 2013 at the age of 65. I miss her and all my old friends and family. I was counting on our shared memories.

So I think aging is about being among the last witnesses to your life events and the life events of those you love. Memories become less reliable, and the 'future,' with its health and other unknown challenges, seems relatively insecure. I am left with this lovely 'present,' the Latin motto Carpe Diem, and fond thoughts of a firm mattress.

"SWIFT AS THE WILD GOOSE FLIES"

Suzanne Adam

The words in the newspaper jump out at me: "All ages. No experience required." Does that include a seventy-year-old woman with stiff joints?

I've always wanted to try kayaking. It suggests adventure and an intimate way to dip my senses into the natural world. I'm long past walking the Pacific Crest Trail, but kayaking? Why not? I read on.

It would be a guided trip across Tomales Bay in Northern California, all equipment provided. Such an expedition requires courage. I need company, so I propose the idea to Martha and Jack, the friends I'm staying with during my visit back to my hometown. To my delight, they agree.

Early Saturday morning, in a veil of fog, we wind along California's Highway One bordering the coast of the bay. Past the town of Marshall, we locate the small boat harbor alongside Nick's Cove, where we meet up with Brett, our young guide. For the next half hour, he patiently explains the gear we'll be wearing: an awkward blue plastic spray skirt hung from suspenders, to be topped by an orange life jacket. He demonstrates how to hold and swing the paddle, how to place our legs, and how to stretch the elasticized rim of the skirt around the kayak's opening. This is going to be more complicated than I expected.

Before us are three kayaks: a needle-thin blue one for Brett, a double and a single one for us.

"Who wants to go in the single?" asks Brett.

I raise my hand. No wimpy double kayaks for me.

The morning mist begins to lift, and the bay waters, smooth as liquid silver, shimmer before us. Like ducklings, we follow Brett northwest toward our destination, a small beach on a peninsula at the opposite shore, home to a herd of tule elk. Farther out, the wind begins to ruffle the bay waters. I slow to view a scattering of ducks and then paddle wildly to catch up with the others. We skim past the tops of oyster beds dotted with scurrying sanderlings that pay no heed to our intrusion.

The farther out into the bay we advance, the stronger whips the wind – and the harder I must exert my sagging biceps. From the corner of my eye, I spot something in the water following me. I turn. Nothing there. Paddle. Right. Left. Right. Left. I turn again. There it is. Big, winsome eyes staring out from a silky, round head. A harbor seal. "Hi there," I call. "Are you spying on me?" The seal plays hide-and-seek until I reach the beach.

Brett yanks our kayaks onto the sand. I wonder how I'll extract myself from my vessel and unfold my cramped legs, but it's surprising what one can do when one's pride is at stake. Finally, in upright position, I wobble toward the table Brett has set up with snacks of local cheese, bread, and strawberries as he explains that the varying vegetation on the bay's opposing sides is due to a fault line running under it.

Needing to stretch my legs, I follow Jack up a nearby hill, where we sight two tule elk. Then, back on the beach, we don our gear for the return.

"Who wants to try the single kayak on the way back?" I ask.

Martha volunteers. I settle into the double one in front of Jack, and we start off. Wow. Sharing the work is a gentle breeze.

Then Martha calls, "I don't feel very stable. I'd like to change back." Returning to shore, I once more angle my body into the single kayak.

Brett announces, "We'll have the wind in our favor, but the tide's against us."

It feels like everything is against us. Brett calls to me, "Try using the rudder." Working the alternating pedals makes the job easier, but

Nick's Cove is just a tiny speck in the distance that isn't getting any bigger. Twist left. Paddle. Pull. Twist right. Paddle. Pull. My sleeves are wet, and I taste salt water in my mouth, but this is what I came for—a challenge and intimacy with this bay on whose shores I splashed as a child, screaming at the sight of transparent jellyfish.

Left paddle. Right paddle. Will the shore ever get closer? I imagine a bowl of hot clam chowder waiting for me at Nick's Cove and push onward, singing aloud an old Girl Scout song: *Our paddles clean and bright, flashing like silver, swift as the wild goose flies. Dip, dip, and swing. Dip, dip, and swing.*

At last. The dock. The tip of my kayak glides onto the ramp where Brett waits. I want to punch my fist into the air with a jubilant "Yes!" I've proven to myself that I'm capable of a demanding physical feat, after years of being overshadowed by my super-athlete husband and sons. Oh, I know I'll never become a Pam Houston, braving the white waters of a wild Colorado River, but I will and can do this again.

Never has clam chowder tasted so good.

A Time For Everything
Ariela Zucker

To me, the year will always start in September.
Summer's end seeps into the
High-Holidays weighty thoughts of repentance, as
The Days of Awe wrap around me a heavy cloak that
Will lift only when the day of final judgment wears away.
Until next year, I repeat it like a mantra.
Until spring returns.
A time to be born, and a time to die,
And it all starts in September.

Always in September,
A sudden trace of coolness in the morning air
& patchy fog evaporates into translucent blue.
And I know that with blazing reds summer will soon die
Then the somber air of autumn's grays, and winter's whites
Heavy on my shoulders, til spring revives.
There is a time to be born; there is a time to die.
And on the way don't we all change our colors,
Just like the seasons do.

RUBY
Janice Airhart

They named her Ruby. We weren't sure we would learn her name before she was born, but I didn't press the issue, and eventually our son and daughter-in-law decided to tell the family what our granddaughter's n ame would be. There was a small amount of fanfare before the "reveal," and I had reason to harbor a bit of premature excitement at the prospect; we were told they'd chosen a name from the family. I didn't suspect they'd choose my name. God, no. But I felt I had slight reason to hope for Barbara Jean. It was my mother's name, and coincidentally was my daughter-in-law's only aunt's name. It must have been popular in the 1920s. Our daughter-in-law's parents were both deceased, so it seemed equally possible they'd choose her mother's name. I would have been okay with that.

Instead, they chose my stepmother's name: Ruby. In the early 2000s, certain old-fashioned names became *de rigueur*, and jewels like Opal, Emerald, and Ruby made a bit of a comeback. The only Rubies I knew of were my stepmother and a couple of entertainers from the '20s. While I was fond of my stepmother, I was bowled over by their choice. Neither my son nor my daughter-in-law seemed particularly close to my stepmother. Of course, she'd been my son's grandmother all his life, but they lived in different states and didn't communicate that often once he married. More to the point, she and I still had a bit of a wary relationship. Maybe it seemed so on my side only, but still.

Ruby Kay Lundgren, widow, married my father when I was 14, about 10 months after my mother's death. She and her three daughters belonged to the same Lutheran church my family had attended nearly all my life. The Lundgren family moved to Lake Charles after Bob Lundgren's death a couple of years before the Henke-Lundgren merger of 1966, as our parents' marriage is referred to even now. I gained three new stepsisters, one of whom was a mere four months older than I and with whom I had become friends. In fact, Dad often said it was their daughters who had brought them together.

In some ways, gaining a mother—even a stepmother—was something I'd hoped for all those years I was without one, while mine was committed to the state mental hospital hours away from our home. This situation was anything but common in our small town in the '50s and '60s, and it made me something of a pariah. Schizophrenia's cause was—and is—not well understood, though theories hinted that the victim's mother was to blame. It seemed it could transfer from mothers to children, due to the mother's odd behavior. My classmates' parents evidently worried I had caught it and that I might infect their own children. When my mother died in 1966, my siblings and I sighed in relief. We would no longer be those kids with the mother in the insane asylum. When our father remarried, we had a *real* mother, a mother who was *normal*.

Fourteen is an awkward age. I was a self-conscious, socially awkward teen, not unlike many other fourteen-year-olds. Transitioning from elementary to junior high school had not been traumatic, since

I moved on with most of the kids I'd been in school with since first grade. But moving to another house, in another part of town in the middle of my last year in junior high school meant transferring to a new school district. I knew no one. It was the most traumatic event of adolescence, more traumatic than my mother's death and more traumatic than learning to live in a new household with new family members.

Things didn't get much better in high school the next year, either. My elementary school chums attended the "other" high school in town.

At the same time, my father seemed to suddenly abdicate his authority as a parent to Ruby. Again, I didn't harbor any ill will toward her—she was my good friend's mother and I liked her a great deal. Yet I grew to resent her position and felt abandoned by my father. I was always conscious that Ruby was *their* mother, and not mine. My stepsisters were her *real* daughters, not me. New household rules were established that I found arbitrary and sometimes confusing. Early experience taught me to be observant and obedient, and I watched carefully to learn how to behave in this new environment. I was determined not to make waves or to be too conspicuous, but it was exhausting.

I never felt at home in *their* home and was almost relieved to find myself pregnant at 18, so that I could marry and start a family of my own. My little family soon moved one state away, then two, returning to our hometown once or twice a year. It took decades for me to appreciate the challenges Ruby must have faced when inheriting three additional teenage children in the merger. She was never deliberately unkind, and had often gone out of her way to treat each of the six of us equally. Yet there was a wall between us, and I did not test its strength for fear of being rejected.

When I learned my granddaughter would be named Ruby, a great many emotions resurfaced, some of them not very charitable. Yet as is my habit, I hid my discomfort. At the time, I thought Ruby was a *horrible* name for an infant. It seemed to belong only to old women who wore garishly colored muumuus and spangly bracelets, dyed their hair burnt sienna, and spoke with oddly foreign accents. Not that my stepmother had done any of those things; she hadn't. But still, Ruby

Josephine seemed an awfully long and complicated name for such a small human.

After more than 10 years, Ruby Jo rolls off the tongue without hesitation. For a while, we referred to "Big Ruby" and "Little Ruby," and I came to find the distinction humorous, as did my stepmother and stepsisters. As is inevitably the case with a child, their personality becomes so enmeshed with their name that it feels as though no other name would fit.

And in some strange way, my granddaughter made it easier for me to relate to my stepmother; I think the connection between us was strengthened. We now simply refer to Ruby Josephine as "Rubes," and it seems a fitting compromise. She appears to appreciate a name that no one else of her acquaintance shares. Her name now fits her as no other could.

Ruby Kay died last year at the age of 93, a few weeks before Ruby Josephine turned 10. I traveled to our hometown in Louisiana a few days before her death, because she'd recently been placed in hospice care. She greeted me happily and, though bedridden, offered me something to eat or drink—always the hostess. She introduced me to her caregiver as "her baby daughter." She had never referred to me this way, and the tears in her eyes when she said it has struck me since as regret over the distance she felt between us. I will carry that with me. I will also be reminded of this woman who was my mother for almost 52 years in new ways, through a granddaughter who bears her name.

FROM THE STARS
Margaret Dubay Mikus

Here I am
naked before you
all scars, weakness,
vulnerability revealed

as beautiful.

Steely resolve,
stubborn determination,
hard-won power

as foundation.

Unashamed,
unassuming,
hiding nothing
I might once have deemed

unacceptable.
Something to be said for
enduring, growing,
transforming, transcending.

Every wrinkle
tells a story
of care or neglect.

Every scar a tale
of chance or choice,
guilt, healing, awareness, or regret.

I can tell you
have come from the stars
just to see

life here in action.
Here I am

THE BEST OF TIMES

Mary Jo Doig

A few years ago, I facilitated several Older Women's Legacy workshops in two local libraries. The OWL workshop is organized into five weekly segments that provide a structure to help each woman tell her unique and important story. For me, personally, older women's legacy writing is so valuable not only for the storyteller, but also her family, her community, and often far beyond. To assist a woman with this exceptional activity can range, in my experience, from a privilege to a sacred activity.

Nancy Virginia signed up for an OWL workshop class. She'd lived in her small Crozet, Virginia, community nearly all of her life and loved telling her endless personal and community stories. She was active in her church as well as many other local associations and events. Her mid-size white car could be seen parked in town on most any day. Her license plate read: ON MY WAY.

Graced with a ninth decade of life, Nancy Virginia's blue eyes often sparkled beneath her short, snowy hair as her gentle voice read one of her stories to us, or responded to another writer's story. Her smile was ever-present, her laughter contagious, her compassion palpable.

Thus opened this singular OWL journey, as each one always is. Our small group of six wrote stories about their lives, shared them, and provided kind feedback to each other. With each story, one or more participants would discover connections with other members. During each successive gathering I could see and feel the ever-deepening bonds developing between the women.

The first week we wrote about "The People Who Shaped Us;" "Memories" in the second week, then "Love and Work" followed. When the fourth week arrived, our focus was on "Lessons of Loss" and "The Best of Times." When I walked into our beautiful library conference room that afternoon, I had no idea I would hear an eight-sentence story that I'd never forget. Or that the story would live on in a way I couldn't imagine.

Nancy Virginia shared the brief, succinct, and poignant story she'd titled, "The Happiest Time of My Life." For several minutes, the gathered women spoke deeply heart-felt comments, then, in conclusion, thanked her. Nancy Virginia glowed in an affirmation of the story she'd just read.

We went on to read the remainder of our stories and share our thoughts. We described, for example, what we liked about each piece, what the most unforgettable sentence was, and how we felt after hearing the story.

Our workshop concluded the following week with the topic "Your Lessons and Your Teachings: What has life taught you? What legacy do you wish to leave?" Again, we wrote, read, shared feelings, and bonded more deeply. Reluctantly we said goodbye. Yet, before we left, Nancy Virginia asked me if she could join another writing group and we soon welcomed her into an ongoing group that still exists today.

There we shared many more of Nancy Virginia's stories, about the history of her community as well as her own life in time and place. One day I asked her, "Are you gathering your stories together somewhere?"

"Oh, yes," she replied with a smile. "My daughters are helping me with that." My exhale was of deep relief.

A mere two weeks later, we received the sad news that Nancy Virginia had passed away with little warning. Her daughters had been with her, and shared that shortly before Nancy Virginia passed on to her next life, she gazed at them, smiled, and murmured, "I'm *so* happy. I'm going home."

Her loss to her family, church, community, and her writing sisters was unfathomable. Because her presence had been so abundant, it was hard to reconcile with the now-empty place in our world that she left.

As I prepared to attend her wake the evening before her funeral, I thought about what I knew of Nancy Virginia's life and our shared time in circles. Then I remembered the small booklet of stories we'd created after her OWL workshop concluded. Through damp eyes, I re-read first her simple, poignant story about September 11, and paused to reflect on many things. Then I turned the page and there was the story she'd written for her fourth OWL gathering: "Lessons of Loss" and "The Best of Times."

I embraced the booklet and carried it with me into the large church, filled to capacity with friends and community. I met Nancy Virginia's daughters and asked if I could show them a story their mom had written. "Oh, yes," they breathed.

I read them the story and shared their quiet tears as they listened. When we were done, one asked to photograph the story. She wanted to read it at her mother's funeral the following day. I held the booklet steady as she snapped several photos.

Unfortunately, I was not physically present at her funeral, but my heart was. It could hear each word beautifully spoken to the packed church pews. It could feel the collective emotions of the listeners. And it could see the tears and reminiscent smiles of all present as they listened to Nancy Virginia's final words about "The Happiest Time in My Life:"

I always longed to be married and wanted a large family. Then I met Kirk and knew he was "it." Our life together became the happiest time of my life. Neither of us knew the secrets of being a good mate, but our commitment carried us through the rough spots of our marriage. As our faith became our strong solid base, our happiness turned into real joy even amidst deep pain. We grew to be less in control and willing to surrender our way, our will, and our control in favor of each other's. We went from the mindset of finding the right person to being the right person. We really did become more other-centered and less self-centered—less of me and more of you.

RETROSPECTIVE

Linda D. Menicucci

From where I sit
On the covered porch of my house
Up on the ridge,
I can see the manzanita and pine trees
In the small valley below.

From where I sit,
I can see the years of my life before me—
The teen who stuffed envelopes for JFK,
The college student who opposed the Vietnam War,
The young mother lost and afraid.

From where I sit,
I can see the years
Of running, crawling, and being dragged
Through the life I lived,
Until I found my strength, walked forward unafraid.

From where I sit,
I can see
Rights that were wronged,
Wrongs that were righted,
And I was a part of it.

From where I sit,
I can see the woman I am today,
Seventy,
And finally,
Happy.

TOWING A JEEP

Maya Lazarus

My friend is 84. Still mobile.
Still lucid. He moved from a decrepit
nursing facility to an assisted living home.
A step up.

The home's owner, a pleasant fellow,
drove my friend to retrieve
his 25-year-old Jeep
stored with a former neighbor.

Last registration sticker, 2011.
That was eight years ago!
The Jeep doesn't work.
They towed it back to the home.

My friend says, *I'll get it fixed.*

Really? And do you have a driver's license?

No, I'll study and take the test again.

I keep silent.

What dreams will I hold fast
when / if I reach 84?

DREAM REFLECTIONS

Carol Toole

In my 30's, I had recurring dreams that my teeth were falling out, sometimes a few, sometimes by the handful. This loss horrified me, and waking from this dream brought deep relief. I have never studied dreams, but I believe such dreams are not uncommon, perhaps representing a threshold of development, a deep cellular change. This particular transition actually happens for each of us around our seventh year when we leave our early childhood behind. As children, we pass through tough stuff indeed, though in the case of teeth, we know a second set awaits us.

In my case, this dream of "sloughing off" was also prescient. As I entered my 40s, my teeth did fall out, at least most of them on the lower left side. I was diagnosed with a mandibular myxoma, a tumor of the jaw. In his office, my surgeon held a skull in his hand as he marked the section of jaw that would be removed. Of course the teeth would be sacrificed. I listened to his description of what would happen to me under the knife; and when he asked if I had questions, I inquired whether the skull was from the last patient on whom he had performed the surgery. Luckily, he had a sense of humor as well as skill, and I had no choice but to go on this strange ride. I learned losing teeth in reality is not nearly so frightening as the dream version; a physical alteration not as dreadful as an interior one, purging the known in one's life to make room for the new.

My 40s brought, along with perimenopause, dreams of losing something more pliable and alive. In these dreams, I held an infant in my arms, feeling the soft, warm weight pressed against my heart as though part of me. Invariably, I would lose the baby, and then seek desperately to recover that which had been in my care. Easy to parallel this with leaving a time of life consumed by caring for children and family, finally embracing a vital part of myself that would surely die if neglected. At this time I struggled to keep my attention on aims long left nascent within me.

The next decade, my 50s, I dream of houses. Place, in the deepest sense of the word, with architecture and landscape: vivid colors on walls, a rambling layout of rooms, a strangely carved mantle framing a fireplace; or particular acreage, where a yard meets asphalt or other houses. Each detail somehow familiar as my limbs, yet with scintillating newness. In these dreams, I am intrigued by the distinct habitation at the same time I grieve for the home I left behind. I had loved my own house, the land and views, so absolutely, why had I chosen to abandon it? The replacement never matches up in the end, almost always a crack in the walls, some annoyance in the yard, neighbors closing in, and no way back. I wonder if these rooms are spaces I have made in myself but have not yet fully inhabited. I stumble, unsure as a toddler who takes those first steps as her world and possibilities become larger.

Deep within life's tide of duties and distractions, an undercurrent flows freely round life forms hidden and mysterious until illuminated by our dreams. Perhaps dreams hold a mirror to waking life, reflecting what's really going on underneath. They show loss and gain: that in the next decade my physical body will wane, yet strength swells within; and when I fear no forward motion, I am, in truth, rolling on gravity's waves toward learning to let go, nurture my core self, expand my tolerance for others, and finally to inhabit spaciousness.

ABOUT THE CONTRIBUTORS

Suzanne Adam – Santiago, Metropolitan, Chile

Suzanne graduated from UC Berkeley, served in the Peace Corps in Colombia, and moved to Santiago, Chile in 1972 to marry her boyfriend, Santiago. She explores this experience in her 2015 memoir, *Marrying Santiago*. Her latest book, *Notes from the Bottom of the World: A Life in Chile*, was published in 2018 by She Writes Press. Her essays have been published in The Christian Science Monitor, California Magazine, Persimmon Tree, and others. She blogs at *tarweedspirit.blogspot.com*.

Janice Airhart – Leander, OK

I am a former medical technologist, journalist, and teacher of science and English. My husband and I recently retired and moved to Texas to be nearer our granddaughter, her parents, and my brother's family. We are enjoying spending time with family and getting acquainted with our new surroundings. I am currently working on a memoir book project about my experiences as the daughter of a schizophrenic.

Pat Anthony – Fontana, KS

Pat writes the backroads, mining characters, relationships, and herself. A recently retired educator and former poetry editor, she holds an MA in Humanities, poems daily, edits furiously, and scrabbles for honesty no matter the cost. Published or forthcoming in Awkward Mermaid, Broadkill Review, Cholla Needles, Heron Tree, and Nature Writing, among others, most recently winning 1st Place in The Blue Nib's mini-chapbook contest for *Pedaling with Mangoes*, which rose to Number One for the UK's chapbook list.

Deborah L. Bean – Rowlett, TX

Deborah is a native Texan raised during the height of the moon race, which piqued her interest in science fiction. In 2016, she completed the **Your Novel Year** program at ASU's Piper Center for Creative Writing. Deborah has had four technical manuals published. Her short story, *Money Doesn't Come in the Mail*, was published in the SCN *Journal*, September 2014. She won 1st Place from the Writers Guild of Texas for her flash fiction, *The Visiting Professor*, in 2016.

Pat Bean – Tucson, AZ

A retired journalist, Pat lives in Tucson with her canine companion, Scamp. She is a wondering-wanderer, avid reader, Lonely Planet Community Pathfinder, Story Circle Network board member, author of *Travels with Maggie*, enthusiastic birder, and is always searching for life's silver lining. She blogs at **https://patbean.net**

Carol J. Wechsler Blatter, LCSW, DCSW – Tucson, AZ

Carol is a psychotherapist in private practice in Tucson. She has received honorable mention from New Millennium Writings for her stories. Her personal essay, *Four Weeks Living With You,* was published in the spring 2019 edition of Chaleur Press. She is a wife, mother, and grandmother. Her clever granddaughter inspires many of her writings. Carol's writing teacher and mentor is author and poet Sheila Bender.

Betsy Boyd – Maryville, TN

Betsy's professional career spanned 40 years as a high school and college writing teacher, Learning Center administrator, college mental health counselor and academic advisor. She has always enjoyed writing and has been a member of Story Circle Network since 2009. Her story, "Jimmy Carter McGill," featuring her rescued Maine Coon, was published in *Chicken Soup for the Soul: Life Lessons from the Cat.* When not writing, Betsy enjoys traveling, needlework, and hiking the Smoky Mountains.

Lisa Braxton – Weymouth, MA

Lisa's debut novel, *The Talking Drum*, is forthcoming from Inanna Publications in Spring 2020. She is a fellow of the Kimbilio Fiction Writers Program and a book reviewer for *2040 Review*. Her stories and essays have appeared in *Vermont Literary Review, Black Lives Have Always Mattered, Chicken Soup for the Soul,* and *The Book of Hope*. She received Honorable Mention in *Writer's Digest's* 84th and 86th annual writing contests in the inspirational essay category. Her website: www.lisabraxton.com.

Lois Ann Bull – Easton, CT

With 78 years to write about, I started with the stories of my grandparents and parents. After self-publishing, I wrote a second book covering my years of motherhood, stories with small children, pets, and horses in the backyard. Book three has the coming of age stories: mistakes, secrets, escapades, of college and graduate school that live in my memory, never shared but part of who I became. This writing experience became a revelation.

Claire Butler – Cincinnati, OH

I have been writing since I was twelve years old. I just finished my first memoir, untitled, which is in its first edit. My second book will be finished before the end of 2019, titled Conversations with the Tuesday Night Girls. I blogged for JenningsWire for about a year, and have had some success with publishing poetry. I live in Cincinnati with my two dogs, where I study French and paint oil on canvas.

Katelynn Butler – Amarillo, TX

I am a teacher and single mother currently residing in the Texas Panhandle. I am a world traveler, a naturalist, and a fighter for social justice. I hope to someday inspire my son to fight for what he believes in with the same passion imbued in my own work. Stories rescue us.

Shelley Johnson Carey – Silver Spring, MD

Shelley is the author of *Thin Mint Memories: Scouting for Empowerment through the Girl Scout Cookie Program.* She works in educational publishing and received her BA from Hampshire College and her MFA in creative nonfiction from Goucher College. While the crunch of a Thin Mint evokes too many wonderful Girl Scout experiences to count, her absolute favorite cookie memories center around tasting the first coconutty Samoa of the cookie season.

Rollyn Carlson – Austin, TX

Born September 21, 1951, I'm just a storyteller and activist for women's rights. I have an undergraduate degree in Psychology from Antioch University. I've had my heart broken, mended, then broken again.

Marilyn H. Collins – Rogers, AR

Marilyn is known for her practical, hands-on workshops. She is author of local/regional history books, writing guides, and magazine articles. Her CHS Publishing Step-by-Step Writing Guides include "Memoir Writing Guide: Brighten Your Leaf on the Family Tree," "You Can Write a Book about Your Family," "Market Yourself, Market Your Book," and "The Art & Business of Writing Local or Regional History." Author. Speaker. Writing/Marketing Coach. Online/Classroom Workshop Instructor. Editor. https://www.marilynhcollins.com

Susan D. Corbin – Austin, TX

Susan retired from the University of Texas, PhD in hand. She is 68 years old, married 47 years to the man she met at 15, mother of 2, and grandmother of 7. This phase of her life is dominated by writing. She self-published a book, *Hallowed Ground, Sacred Space*, from a Rick Diamond Bible study. Her piece here is the introduction to her next book, *Get your Dissertation Done and Stay Sane.*

Mary Jo Doig – Afton, VA

Mary Jo is a 20-year Story Circle Network member, who deeply values life-writing. She is a facilitator of Women's Life-Writing & Older Women's Legacy (OWL) Workshops. She published her memoir "Patchwork: A Memoir of Love and Loss" in 2018. For more information about Mary Jo, or to read her blog, or contact her, go to her website: www.maryjodoig.com.

Debra Dolan – Vancouver, BC, Canada

Debra has been a member of SCN for ten years. She leads a quiet and uncomplicated life on the west coast of Canada where she can often be found walking for miles in search of rain on glorious sunny days. Debra is an avid reader of women's memoir and a private journaler for over 50 years.

Sara Etgen-Baker – Anna, TX

Sara's love for words began when her mother read the dictionary to her every night. A teacher's unexpected whisper, "You've got writing talent," ignited her writing desire. She ignored that whisper and pursued a different career, but eventually she re-discovered her inner writer and began writing memoirs and essays, many of which have been published in anthologies and magazines, including *Wisdom Has a Voice, Chicken Soup for the Soul, Guideposts*, and *Times They Were A Changing.*

Sarah Fine – Toronto, ON, Canada

I am an enthusiastic writer, a happily retired teacher/social worker, and the proud mother of three amazing adult children. I enjoy life in the Beaches on the shore of Lake Ontario with my interesting and supportive spouse and a richness of friends. I am grateful for each day!

Susan Flemr – Des Moines, IA

Susan spends her retirement from nursing and ordained ministry with her husband Bill in Des Moines. She relishes time to read, write, and play her cello. Each and every day she's filled with gratitude for the privilege of growing older, with its challenges and its joys.

Jeanne Baker Guy – Cedar Park, TX

Jeanne operates Jeanne Guy Gatherings as an author, speaker, seasoned facilitator, and has been a self-awareness "re-story" writing coach since 1994. She is SCN's 2018-2020 president. Jeanne is co-author of *Seeing Me: a guide to reframing the way you see yourself through reflective writing.* She is completing a memoir, *You'll Never Find Us,* the story of how her children were stolen from her and how she stole them back. You should pre-order the book. http://www.jeanneguy.com

Ann Haas – Mogadore, OH

I am a certified legacy writer/facilitator, who has taught legacy writing at the local, state and national levels, most recently at the Dayton, Ohio Alzheimer's Association annual conference. In addition to establishing the legacy writing program and training volunteers at our local hospice, I specialize in short-form legacy writing methods using blessings, six-word memoirs, reverse bucket lists, en plein air nature writing and a storytelling method using a three-question memoir format.

Jazz Jaeschke Kendrick – Austin, TX

Jazz responds to the world around her through poetry, augmented by photography and collage. Her work can be found at www. StepsAndPauses.Wordpress.com. Jazz also facilitates SCN's poetry circle, writing e-circle 4. She is Austin-based but roams extensively with husband Gary, camping in their Airstream.

Shawn LaTorre – Austin, TX

Shawn is a writer from Austin, Texas. She is married and has three children, two cats, one sailboat, and several quilts. When she is not in Austin, she can be found in the windy city of Chicago, sailing the Great Lakes, or climbing mountains in Colorado. A former middle and high school teacher, Shawn is now retired and a board member for Story Circle Network.

Maya Lazarus – Caldwell, TX

Maya moved to central Texas five years ago from the East Coast and lives on five acres with her husband and four dogs. Now retired, she enjoys journal-writing, flash fiction/non-fiction, haiku and free-verse poetry. She recently self-published a memoir, *Through the Rabbit Hole: One Family's Bipolar Success Story*, to give hope to other parents who have a child with a mental health condition.

Jane Gragg Lewis – Laguna Niguel, CA

No one wants to sit and listen to my stories! That was my reason to join a writing group about eight years ago. The few childhood memories I wanted to write for my daughters and grandchildren morphed into a book, *A Jar of Fireflies*, a memoir about growing up in the South. Before joining SCN, I wrote an ESL activity text, *Dictation Riddles*. I've also been very lucky to have quite a few stories appear in various publications.

Juliana Lightle – Canyon, TX

From a family farm in Missouri, Juliana became a singer, college administrator, corporate manager, racehorse breeder and trainer, educator, and author. She earned a PhD in counseling and business. Currently, she teaches high school Spanish and English, raises horses, writes and sings in the Texas Panhandle. Published works include a book on sexual harassment, and a memoir in poetry, *On the Rim of Wonder*. Next is *You're Gonna Eat That?! Adventures with Food, Family, and Friends,* to be published in 2019.

Claire McCabe – Elkton, MD

Claire teaches creative writing at the University of Delaware, where she is faculty advisor for the student literary annual. McCabe earned Bachelor's degrees in Journalism and Literature from Virginia Commonwealth University. She holds a Master's in Linguistics from the University of Delaware, and an MFA in Creative Writing: Poetry from the Solstice Program at Pine Manor College. She splits her time between homes in Newark, Delaware, and Fairhill, Maryland.

Linda D. Menicucci, PhD – Paradise, CA

Linda is a licensed Clinical Psychologist. She practiced in San Francisco for over twenty years and specializes in Analytical Psychology, Dream Analysis, and the Psychology of Women. She and her husband relocated to Paradise, California, in 2001 and never looked back. The 2018 fire destroyed much but not their love for the foothills. They remain in Paradise. She has one son and one grandson, the love of her life.

Margaret Dubay Mikus, PhD – Lake Forest, IL

Margaret was a research scientist and teacher, who healed from multiple sclerosis and breast cancer. Now a poet, singer, photographer, and storyteller, she is the author of four books of poetry. Her CD has selected poems and three original songs. In 2013 she was the Illinois Featured Author for the *Willow Review*. Margaret created a writing guide from her popular poem, "I Am Willing." Her blog, including 62 poem-videos, is at www.FullBlooming.com.

Marilea C. Rabasa – Camano Island, WA

I grew up in Massachusetts. For seventeen years I was an ESL teacher in Virginia. Before that, I lived overseas in the Foreign Service. Just as I provided "springboards" for my students in writing class, my travels provide the backdrop for my award-winning debut memoir, *A Mother's Story: Angie Doesn't Live Here Anymore*; and for my second book, *Stepping Stones: A Memoir of Addiction, Loss, and Transformation,* to be published in June 2020.

Sarah Byrn Rickman – Colorado Springs, CO

A former journalist and a licensed Sport pilot, Sarah is the multi-award-winning author of nine books about the WASP (Women Airforce Service Pilots) of WWII. Her latest two are aimed at the YA market: *BJ Erickson WASP Pilot* (2019 Sarton winner) and *Nancy Love: WASP Pilot*. Number 10 is in the works. Sarah holds a BA in English from Vanderbilt University and an MA in creative writing from Antioch University, McGregor. Website: www.sarahbyrnrickman.com.

Marlene B. Samuels, PhD – Chicago, IL

Marlene Samuels holds her PhD and MA from University of Chicago, where she serves on the Graduate School Advisory Counsel. A research sociologist and instructor, her current research addresses female-to-female relational aggression. Marlene is editor and coauthor of *The Seamstress: A Memoir of Survival* and author of *When Digital Isn't Real: Fact Finding Off-Line for Serious Writers*. She divides her time between Chicago and Sun Valley, Idaho.

Nancilynn Saylor – Austin, TX

Following a long career in healthcare and management, I now am blissfully retired. My days are filled with writing, crafting hand-made journals, and adventures in my kitchen. I live in Austin with my forever Romeo and our small chihuahua, Chica.

Madeline Sharples – Manhattan Beach, CA

Madeline is the author of *Leaving the Hall Light On: A Mother's Memoir of Living with Her Son's Bipolar Disorder and Surviving His Suicide*. She also co-authored *Blue-Collar Women: Trailblazing Women Take on Men-Only Jobs,* and wrote the poems for *The Emerging Goddess* photograph book. Aberdeen Bay published her first novel, *Papa's Shoes: A Polish shoemaker and his family settle in small-town America,* a work of historical fiction, in April 2019. Her website: http://madelinesharples.com

Penelope Starr – Tucson, AZ

Author of *The Radical Act of Community Storytelling: Empowering Voices in Uncensored Events*, Penelope is a writer, founder of Odyssey Storytelling in Tucson, workshop facilitator, mixed media artist, and restorer of Navajo rugs. The phrase "lifelong learner" is her mantra. Her current passion is finishing her first novel by July 2020, her 75th birthday. You can see what she is up to at http://penelopestarr.com.

Carol Toole – Dripping Springs, TX

Carol, a Waldorf educator, literacy teacher, and parent educator, has always loved children and language. Her articles have appeared in *Renewal* magazine and other education/parenting publications. Whether processing experiences through writing, playing with language in her classes, or practicing calligraphy, words are always central. She is keenly interested in speech development in young children, currently writing about how enlivened speech helps keep us all in the present moment.

Jo Virgil – Austin, TX

Jo recently retired from a career in journalism and community relations. She has a Master of Journalism degree with a minor in Environmental Science, reflecting her love of writing and appreciation of nature, and has had stories and poetry published in various books, newspapers, magazines, and journals, including Story Circle Network's journals and anthologies. Jo is also an editor for SCN and a board member. She lives by the mantra "Stories are what make us matter."

Jude Walsh – Dayton, OH

Jude is the author of *Post-Divorce Bliss: Ending Us and Finding Me* (Morgan James Press, 2019). She is also a creativity and life coach. Her work has appeared in numerous literary magazines and anthologies including the *Chicken Soup for the Soul* series and *The Magic of Memoir* (She Writes Press, 2016). She is a proud member of Story Circle Network and grateful for all they do to support women's writing. http://www.secondbloomcoaching.com

Bonnie Watkins – Austin, TX

Bonnie has published numerous educational and parenting articles in various journals, as well as memoir and poetry in SCN Journals, along with three stories in *Kitchen Table Stories*. Her first published book is *Little White Church in the Vale: Reflections on Small Town Faith*, which includes her original photography of small town Texas churches.

Mary Jo West – San Clemente, CA

I started writing at age 72, and have been immersed in the process for eight years. I have published my memoir, *Without Reservations*, and a recipe book, *A Little Bit of This and a Little Bit of That*. I've won several poetry awards from California State Poetry Society and the Laguna Beach Poetry Contest. Married for 61 years, with three daughters and nine grandchildren, I've lived in San Clemente for 38 years. Writing is my new adventure.

Marjorie Witt – Lafayette, CA

Marjorie, a member of Story Circle Network for nearly twenty years, blogs in random intervals at https://wittbits.com. Her work has also appeared in *Story Circle Journal*, Street Spirit (Justice News & Homeless Blues in the Bay Area) and talkingsoup.com. Other than working full time, raising a grandson, and reigning over her local Red Hat Society Chapter, Marjorie spends her time fine-tuning her someday-to-be-published memoir, working-titled *Homeless Bound*.

Charlotte Wlodkowski – Pittsburgh, PA

Six years ago, I joined the Millvale Writing Group, and two years later, joined Story Circle Network. I realized I enjoyed creating characters with backgrounds and stories. My belief is that reading, and writing, are basic needs to keep our minds sharp and give us an outlet for expression. It's a pleasure to share my writings.

Jeanne Zeeb-Schecter – Valley Village, CA

I have been a Homeopathic doctor for the past twenty-five years and am now retiring. I belong to a local poetry and writing class, and teach a Creative Life Writing class. I joined SCN three years ago. Currently, I am writing a nonfiction book on Homeopathy and Grief, as well as a historical novel. I am blessed to be married, have a daughter, four granddaughters, and six great-grandchildren.

Ariela Zucker – Ellsworth, ME

Born in Jerusalem, my husband and I left Israel in September, 2001. Followed by three of our daughters, we decided to stay in Maine. Over the summer we live in Ellsworth, in the motel we own and operate. During the winter, we reside in Auburn, and I can dedicate my time to writing and traveling.

ABOUT THE EDITOR

Susan F. Schoch, editor of *Real Women Write: Growing / Older*, is a freelance writer and editor specializing in personal history. She is author of *The Clay Connection,* a study of ceramic artists Jim and Nan McKinnell, for the American Museum of Ceramic Art. She serves on the Board of Story Circle Network, reviews writing by and about women at Story Circle Book Reviews, and edited the 2017 SCN essay collection, *Inside and Out.* She has been editor of the annual *Real Women Write* anthology since 2014. Susan lives in Colorado with her husband, a ceramic artist and teacher. They have a large and loving family.

ABOUT STORY CIRCLE NETWORK:
FOR WOMEN WITH STORIES TO TELL
by Susan Wittig Albert

> We learn best to listen to our own voices if we are listening
> at the same time to other women, whose stories, for all our
> differences, turn out, if we listen well, to be our stories also.
> — *Barbara Deming*

I'm going to use the personal pronoun when I tell you about SCN, because I am its founder and a current member of this wonderful organization. I am very proud of—and often amazed by—all we have done and continue to do.

Chartered in 1997 as a nonprofit organization, SCN is now twenty-two years old and still growing. Over the years, nearly 4,000 women in this country and elsewhere in the world have been members, and many times that number have participated in our programs. Our activities are funded by annual membership dues and fee-based programs, as well as the generous gifts and grants of friends and supporters. Our work is done by a very small paid staff and dozens of volunteers.

Story Circle Network is dedicated to helping women share the stories of their lives and to raising public awareness of the importance of women's personal histories. We carry out our mission through publications, websites, award programs, online and face-to-face classes and workshops, writing and reading circles, blogs, and many woman-focused activities. We sponsor a biannual national women's writing conference, weekend writing retreats called "LifeLines," and a regular program of online classes. We sponsor Story Circle Book Reviews, the largest and oldest women's book review site on the Internet, and the annual Sarton Women's Writing Awards.

We encourage our members to publish their writing through our quarterly *Story Circle Journal*, annual *Real Women Write* anthology, and blogs ("Herstories" and "One Woman's Day"). In addition, SCN has published four collections of members' and others' writing: *With Courage and Common Sense: Memoirs from the Older Women's Legacy Circle*;

What Wildness is This: Women Write about the Southwest, Kitchen Table Stories, and *Inside and Out.*

But what I have just told you about what we are doing at SCN today is likely to be out of date tomorrow, for we continue to explore new ways to serve the growing community of women writers and those who are interested in documenting and celebrating women's lives. To that end, we have created a new and better website, which will be unveiled in 2020.

Meanwhile, I invite you to visit www.storycircle.org, our central website, and from there, explore the many activities SCN has created to support women with stories to tell. We're here to help, because we believe in women's stories. Please join us.

BOOKS PUBLISHED BY STORY CIRCLE NETWORK

Inside and Out: Women's Truths, Women's Stories
edited by Susan F. Schoch

Kitchen Table Stories
edited by Jane Ross

Starting Points
by Susan Wittig Albert

True Words from Real Women, the SCN Anthology, 2009-2014
edited by Amber Lea Starfire, Mary Jo Doig, Susan F. Schoch

Real Women Write: Sharing Our Stories, Sharing Our Lives,
the SCN Anthology, 2015-2019
edited by Susan F. Schoch

What Wildness Is This: Women Write About the Southwest
edited by Susan Wittig Albert, Susan Hanson,
Jan Epton Seale, Paula Stallings Yost

With Courage and Common Sense:
Memoirs from the Older Women's Legacy Circle
edited by Susan Wittig Albert and Dayna Finet

Writing From Life
by Susan Wittig Albert

...by, for, and about women.

"Sometimes it's not the book.
It's where the reader is on her journey."

— *Susan Wittig Albert*

This book was designed using
Proxima Nova, Eccentric, and Adobe Garamond.
Designed and typeset by Sherry Wachter:
sherry@sherrywachter.com

Made in the USA
Coppell, TX
19 September 2020

38285875R00085